Priests, Women, and Families

GW01057525

Jules Michelet

Alpha Editions

This edition published in 2024

ISBN 9789362097248

Design and Setting By

Alpha Editions

www.alphaedis.com

Email - info@alphaedis.com

Contents

EDITOR'S PREFACE.

When it was first proposed to publish an English Translation of this admirable work, its gifted Author wrote to the Translator to the following effect: "This work cannot be without interest to the people of England, among whom, at this moment, the Jesuits are so madly pursuing their work. Nothing is more strange than their chimerical hopes of speedily converting England."

Indeed, their intrigues and manoeuvres were thought at that time— 1845—to be "chimerical," even by many who were *forced* to join in the Jesuit Crusade. One of the Bishops, directed by Dr. Wiseman to use the "Litany for the Conversion of England," replied, "You may as well pray that the blackamoor may be made white." He was ordered to Rome, and six months' detention there quieted his opposition to the Jesuit schemes intended to "bend or break" his country.

In presenting a New Issue of "PRIESTS, WOMEN, AND FAMILIES", we meet a want—a necessity—of Society. The CONFESSIONAL UNMASKED, which so *faithfully* portrayed the Romish and Ritualistic Priest, and which was so unjustly and *illegally* suppressed by the violence and intrigues of Priests and those whom they "directed," was too plain in its utterances for general reading. Its *testimony* as a WITNESS *was* and *is* of the highest importance; but we fully concur with the Author of this "work of art" that it should not be disfigured by the portraits of Priests.

The following *Illustrations* are a proof that something ought to be done on behalf of the deluded creatures who, under the pretence of becoming the "Brides of Christ," are subjected to "indignities" and cruelty, not tolerated anywhere else.

"ARTICLES OF PIETY;"
OR, INSTRUMENTS OF TORTURE IN ENGLISH CONVENTS.

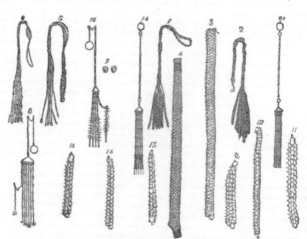

This Engraving is copied from a *Photograph,* Published by the Society. For a description of these and other "Articles of Piety," see *Oxford and Roman Railway.* Price 1s.

This engraving is copied from a *Photograph*, Published by the Society. For a description of these and other "Articles of Piety," see *Oxford and Roman Railway*. Price 1s.

Instruments of Torture are *now* practised upon Nuns in Romish Convents in *London* and in all parts of the country.

The Romish "Articles of Piety," named on the next page, were bought at "Little's Ecclesiastical Warehouse", 20, Cranbourne Street, and at the Convent of the "Sisters of the Assumption of the Perpetual Adoration of the Blessed Sacrament," London.

Such Instruments of Torture are fitter for the worshippers of Baal, than for the worshippers of God; and a person using them upon cattle would lay himself open to a prosecution by the "Society for Prevention of Cruelty to Animals." Both the parties who purchased these articles are intimately known to Mr. Steele, the Secretary of the Protestant Evangelical Mission and Electoral Union.

COPIES OF BILLS GIVEN TO PURCHASERS.

No. 1. Jan. 15, 1868.

Ecclesiastical Warehouse,

20, Cranbourne Street.

                       s. d.

To Hair Shirt 12 6

To Discipline 4 0

Two Do., had last week 3 6

To Massive Waist Chain 8 6

Two Armlets, 3s. 6d. & 1s. 6d.   5 0

One Hair Band 5 0

                £1 18 6

Rec. C. Cuddon. for F. A. LITTLE

No. 2. Convent of the Assumption,
     24, Kensington Sq.

                       s. d.

One Iron Discipline 7 0

One Nut 2 6

       Total 9 6

Rec. Sr. M. Bernardine, May 1, 1869.

No. 3. Convent of the Assumption,

24, Kensington Sq.

	s.	d.
Iron Discipline	5	6
Two Bracelets	1	6
One Nut	2	6
	9	6

Paid S--: Sep. --, 1869.

No. 4. Little's Ecclesiastical
Warehouse, 20, Cranbourne Street.

	s.	d.
To Discipline (9 tails)	6	6
" Ditto (7 tails)	2	3
" Chain Band	6	6
Ditto Smaller	4	6
	19	9

Received with thanks, Sep. --, 1869.

Christian Reader,—It is your duty to testify, on God's behalf, against the *Blasphemy* and *Cruelty* of Romanism. The *Maker* and *Preserver* of man is the loving *Father* who gave His only begotten Son to die for us; and thus make atonement for our sin. "By Him all that believe are justified from all things."—Acts xiii. 38, 39; Micah vi. 6-8; John iii. 16; Rom. iii. 20-26; Heb. ix. 22.

IRON DISCIPLINES OF "THE CHURCH."

Saint Liguori, the Doctor of the Romish Church, commends the use of *Disciplines* to the "True Spouse of Christ" thus:—

"*Disciplines*, or *Flagellations*, are a species of mortification, strongly recommended by St. Francis de Sales, and universally adopted in Religious Communities of both sexes. All the modern Saints, without a single exception, have continually practised this sort of penance. It is related of St. Lewis Gonzaga, that he often scourged himself into blood three times a-day. And at the point of death, not having sufficient strength to use the lash, he besought the Provincial to have him disciplined from head to foot."

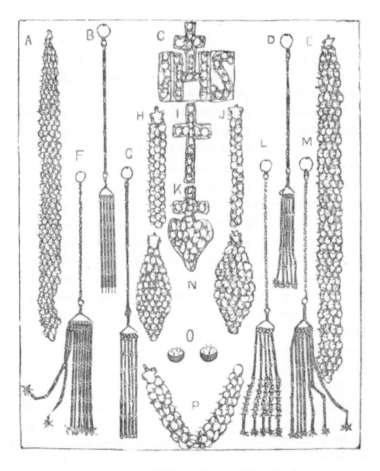

Instruments of Discipline or Flagellation

A. This is a band for going round the body to "mortify the flesh." It is made of *Iron wire*, and the *ends* of each link form Spikes which range in length from the sixteenth of an inch to half an inch.

B. This is a *Flagellum*, made of strong iron wire. It has *five* tails to represent the "Five wounds;" and at the end of each tail there is a *Spike*, about an inch long, to *pierce* the flesh. It will be seen that the lowermost joints are the heaviest, so as to increase the severity of the blows.

C. This is a *Cross* resting upon an "I. H. S."—Jesus the Saviour of Man. It is for wearing on the breast, and is made of *iron*, as, indeed, all the other articles represented in the engraving are. It is covered over with *spikes* on the side next the body.

D. This is another *Flagellum*, commemorative of the "Five wounds." At the end of each tail there is a kind of *Rowel* with sharp points. It is impossible to use this without cutting the flesh.

E. This *Belt* is similar to A, but of stronger material. This *belt* sometimes becomes *imbedded* in the flesh of the devoted *victim* of "the Church."

F. This *Flagellum* has *Nine* tails, to represent the nine months during which "The Word was made flesh." The "Cat-and-nine-tails" and the "Incarnation"!!

G. This *Flagellum* is a modification of B, D, and L.

H, J, P. These are *Bands* for the *limbs*, and, like A and E, are covered with *spikes*.

I. This is a *Cross* similar to that resting upon the "I. H. S." above.

K. This is a *Cross* and *Heart* to be worn over the seat of the affections, to show that all "natural affection" is to be crucified. This was painfully illustrated in the case of a young lady who had left her home and entered one of these Conventual Establishments to the great grief of her parents. Her father called at the convent to see her. She was brought to him, and on his expostulating with her, and soliciting her return home, he observed that she pressed her hands against her breast, and seemed to suffer excruciating pain. After a little, blood oozed through her dress, and she was then withdrawn by the "Sisters."

L. This *Flagellum* may be called the Mother Superior's "*Wild Cat*."

M. This *Flagellum* has Seven tails, to represent the "Seven Dolours" of the Virgin; and a doleful tale they tell.

N. These two *Nets* of Iron wire, covered over with *spikes*, are for the most cruel and immodest purposes. We dare not describe them.

O. Each of these two hemispheres, together forming a *Nut*, has *five brass spikes*, which are used for imprinting the *Stigmata* or "Five wounds" of Christ upon the *Religious*.

Were such cruelties perpetrated upon the *Heathen*, all our *Christian* Churches would resound with appeals to the sympathy of the people to come to the help of the sufferers, whether *Fanatics* or *Victims*. This would be commendable. Why, then, is the same course not adopted on behalf of Nuns, who, as Rev. Pierce Connelly says, "are not only slaves, but who are, *de facto*, by a Satanic consecration, secret prisoners for life, and may any day be put an end to, or much worse, with less risk of vengeance here in England than in Italy or Spain!"—Extracted from the Annual Report of the Protestant Evangelical Mission and Electoral Union, January, 1873.

PREFACE.

The following pages—intended to restore *Domestic Life* to French Society—formed the Preface to the Third Edition of *Priests, Women, and Families*, by M. Michelet, of which celebrated work, "THE PROTESTANT EVANGELICAL MISSION" have published an Edition in English.

This book has produced upon our adversaries an effect we had not anticipated. It has made them lose every sense of propriety and self-respect:—nay, more, even that respect for the sanctuary which it was their duty to teach us. From the pulpits of their crowded churches they preach against a living man, calling him by his name, and invoking upon the author and his book the hatred of those who know not how to read, and who will never read this work. The heads of the clergy must, indeed, have felt themselves touched to the quick, to let loose these furious preachers upon us.

We have hit the mark too fairly, it should seem. Woman!—this was the point on which they were sensitive. Direction, the spiritual guidance of women, is the vital part of ecclesiastical authority; and they will fight for it to the death. Strike, if you will, elsewhere, but not here. Attack the dogma—all well and good; they may, perhaps, make a show of violence, or perpetrate some empty declamation; but if you should happen to meddle with this particular point, the thing becomes serious, and they no longer contain themselves. It is a sad sight to see pontiffs, elders of the people, gesticulating, stamping, foaming at the mouth, and gnashing their teeth.[1] Young men, do not look; epileptic convulsions have occasionally a contagious effect upon the spectators. Let us leave them and depart; we must resume our studies without loss of time: "Art is long, life is short."

I remember having read in the correspondence of Saint Charles Borromeo, that one of his friends, a person of authority and importance, having censured some Jesuit or other who was too fond of confessing nuns, the latter came in a fury to insult him. The Jesuit knew his strength: being a preacher then in vogue, well off at court, and still better at the court of Rome, he thought he need not stand upon ceremony. He went to the greatest extremes, was violent, insolent, as much as he pleased: his grave censor remained cool. The Jesuit could no longer keep within the bounds of decency, and made use of the vilest expressions. The other, calm and firm, answered nothing; he let him continue his declamation, threats, and violent gestures; he only looked at his feet. "Why were you always looking at his feet?" inquired an eye-witness, as soon as the Jesuit, was gone.

"Because," replied the noble man calmly, "I fancied I saw the cloven hoof peeping out every now and then; and this man, who seemed possessed with a devil, might be the tempter himself, disguised as a Jesuit."

One prelate predicts in sorrow that we are sending the priests to martyrdom.

Alas, this martyrdom is what they themselves demand, either aloud or in secret, namely—marriage.

We think, without enumerating the too well known inconveniences of their present state, that if the priest is to advise the family, it is good for him to know what a family is; that as a married man, of a mature age and experience, one who has loved and suffered, and whom domestic affections have enlightened upon the mysteries of moral life, which are not to be learned by guessing, he would possess at the same time more affection and more wisdom.

It is true the defenders of the clergy have lately drawn such a picture of marriage, that many persons perhaps will henceforth dread the engagement. They have far exceeded the very worst things that novelists and modern socialists have ever said against the *legal union*. Marriage, which lovers imprudently seek as a confirmation of love, is, according to them, but a warfare: we marry in order to fight. It is impossible to degrade lower the virtue of matrimony. The sacrament of union, according to these doctors, is useless, and can do nothing unless a third party be always present between the partners—*i.e.*, the combatants—to separate them.

It had been generally believed that two persons were sufficient for matrimony: but this is all altered; and we have the new system, as set forth by themselves, composed of three elements: 1st, *man*, the strong, the violent; 2ndly, *woman*, a being naturally weak; 3rdly, the *priest*, born a man, and strong, but who is kind enough to become weak and resemble woman; and who, participating thus in both natures, may interpose between them.

Interpose! interfere between two persons who were to be henceforth but one! This changes wonderfully the idea which, from the beginning of the world, has been entertained of marriage.

But this is not all; they avow that they do not pretend to make an impartial interference that might favour each of the parties, according to reason. No, they address themselves exclusively to the wife: she it is whom they undertake to protect against her natural protector. They offer to league with her in order to transform the husband. If it were once firmly established that marriage, instead of being unity in two persons, is a league of one of them with a stranger, it would become exceedingly scarce. Two to one! the game would seem too desperate; few people would be bold enough to face the peril. There would be no marriages but for money; and these are already too numerous. People in difficulties would doubtless not fail to marry; for instance, a merchant placed by his pitiless creditor between marriage and a warrant.

To be transformed, re-made, remodelled, and changed in nature! A grand and difficult change! But there would be no merit in it, if it was not of one's free will, and only brought about by a sort of domestic persecution, or household warfare.

First of all, we must know whether transformation means amelioration, whether it be intended by transformation to ascend higher and higher in moral life, and become more virtuous and wise. To ascend would be well and good; but if it should be to fall lower?

And first of all, the wisdom they offer us does not imply knowledge. "What is the use of knowledge and literature? They are mere toys of luxury, vain and dangerous ornaments of the mind, both strangers to the soul." Let us not contest the matter, but pass over this empty distinction that opposes the mind to the soul, as if ignorance was innocence, and as if they could have the gifts of the soul and heart with a poor, insipid, idiotic literature!

But where is their heart? Let us catch a glimpse of it. How is it that those who undertake to develope it in others dispense with giving any proof of it in themselves? But this living fountain of the heart is impossible to be hidden, if we really have it within us. It springs out in spite of everything; if you were to stop it on one side, it would run out by the other. It is more difficult to be confined than the flowing of great rivers:—try to shut up the sources of the Rhone or Rhine! These are vain metaphors, and very ill-placed, I allow: to what deserts of Arabia must I not resort to find more suitable ones?

We are in a church: see the crowd, the dense mass of people who after having wandered far, enter here weary and athirst, hoping to find some refreshment; they wait with open mouths. Will there even be one small drop of dew?

No; a decent, proper, blunt-looking man ascends the pulpit: he will not affect them; he confines himself to proofs. He makes a grand display of reasoning, with high logical pretensions and much solemnity in his premises. Then come sudden, sharp conclusions; but for middle term there is none: "These things require no proof." Why, then, miserable reasoner, did you make so much noise about your proofs?

Well! do not prove! only love! and we will let you off everything else. Say only one word from the heart to comfort this crowd. All that variegated mass of living heads, that you see so closely assembled around your pulpit are not blocks of stone, but so many living souls. Those yonder are young men, the rising generation, our future society. They are of happy dispositions, full of spirit, fresh and entire, such as God made them, and untamed; they rush forward incautiously even to the very brink of precipices. What! youth, danger, futurity, and hopes clouded with fear—does not all this move you? Will nothing open your fatherly heart?

Mark, too, that brilliant crowd of women and flowers: in all that splendour so delightful to the eye there is much suffering. I pray you to speak one word of comfort to them. You know they are your daughters, who come every evening so forlorn to weep at your feet. They confide in you, and tell you everything; you know their wounds. Try to find some consoling word—surely that cannot be so difficult. What man is there who, in seeing the heart of a woman bleeding before him, would not feel his own heart inspired with words to heal it? A dumb man, for want of words, would find what is worth more, a flood of tears!

What shall we say of those who, in presence of so many desponding, sickly, and confiding persons, give them, as their only remedy, the spirit of an academy, glittering commonplaces, old paradoxes, Bonaparteism, socialism, and what not? There is in all this, we must confess, a sad dryness and a great want of feeling.

Ah! you *are* dry and harsh! I felt this the other day (it was in December last), when I read on the walls, as I was passing by, an order from the archbishop. It was a case of suicide; a poor wretch had killed himself in the church of Saint-Gervais. Was it misery, passion, madness, spleen, or moral weakness in this melancholy season? No cause was mentioned; the body alone was there with the blood on the marble slabs; but no explanation. By what gradation of griefs, disappointments, and anguish had he been induced to commit this unnatural act? What steps of moral purgatory had he descended before he reached the bottom of the abyss? Who could say? No one. But any man with a gleam of imagination in his heart, sees in this solemn mystery something to make him weep and pray. That man is not Mr. Affre: read the mandate. There is compassion for the blood-stained church, and pity for the polluted stones; but for the dead only a malediction. But, whether a Christian or not, guilty or not, is he not still a man, my lord bishop? Could you not, whilst you were condemning suicide, let fall one word of pity by the way? No, no sentiment of humanity, nothing for the poor soul, which, besides its misfortune (which must have been terrible, indeed, since it could not support it), departs all alone and accursed, to attempt that perilous flight of the other life and judgment.

Another very different fact had given me some time before a similar impression. I had gone on business to the house of the venerable Sister * * *.

She was absent; and two persons, a lady and an aged priest, were waiting, like myself, in the small parlour. The lady seemed actuated by some motive of beneficence: the priest, as they are lords and masters in every Religious house, seemed to be quite at home, and, to beguile the time, was writing letters at the sister's bureau. At the conclusion of every note, he listened to the lady for a moment. The latter, whose gentle face bore traces of grief, impressed one at once with the goodness of her disposition: perhaps she would not have attracted my attention, but there was something in her that interested me. Was it passion or grief? I overheard without listening—she had lost her son.

An only son, full of affection, spirits, and courage; a young hero, who, leaving the Polytechnic school, had abandoned everything, riches, high life, pleasure, happiness, and such a mother! And regardless alike of safety and danger, had rushed to Marseilles, thence to Algiers, to the enemy, and to death.

The poor woman, wholly occupied with this idea, snatched, from time to time, a little moment to put in a word; she wanted to speak to him, and appeal to his compassion. The scene was infinitely touching and natural, without any theatrical effect. Her moderate grief and sighs, without tears, affected me the more.

She was evidently wasting her breath. The thoughts of the priest were elsewhere. It was not possible for him not to listen; he was forced to say something or other (the lady was rich, and her carriage was waiting at the door); but he got off as cheap as he could: "Yes, Madam, Providence tries us. It strikes us for our good. These are very painful trials," &c., &c. Such vague and cold words did not discourage the lady; she drew her chair nearer, thinking he would hear her better: "Ah! Sir, how shall I tell you? Ah! how can you understand so heavy a calamity?" She would have made a dead man weep.

Did you ever see the heart-rending sight of the poor pointer, that has been wounded by a shot, writhing at his master's feet, and licking his hands, as if praying to him to help him? The comparison will appear, perhaps, strange to those who have not seen the reality. However, at that moment, I felt it in my heart. That woman, mortally wounded, yet so gentle in her grief, seemed to be writhing at the feet of the priest, and to entreat his compassion.

I looked at that priest: he was vulgar and unfeeling, such as we see so often, neither wicked nor good; there was nothing to indicate a heart of iron, but he was as if made of wood. I saw plainly that no one word of all which his ear had received had entered his soul. One sense was wanting. But why torment a blind man by speaking to him of colours? He answers vaguely; occasionally he may guess pretty nearly; but how can it be helped? he cannot see.

And do not think that the feelings of the heart can be guessed at more easily. A man without wife or child might study the mysterious working of a family in books and the world for ten thousand years, without ever knowing one word about them. Look at these men; it is neither time, opportunity, nor facility that they lack to acquire knowledge; they pass their lives with women who tell them more than they tell their husbands; they know and yet they are ignorant: they know all a woman's acts and thoughts, but they are ignorant precisely of what is the best and most intimate part of her character, and the very essence of her being. They hardly understand her as a lover (of God or man), still less as a wife, and not at all as a mother. Nothing is more painful than to see them sitting down awkwardly by the side of a woman to caress her child: their manner towards it is that of flatterers or courtiers—anything but that of a father.

What I pity most in the man condemned to celibacy is not only the privation of the sweetest joys of the heart, but that a thousand objects of the natural and moral world are, and ever will be, a dead letter to him. Many have thought, by living apart, to dedicate their lives to science; but the reverse is the case: in such a morose and crippled life science is never fathomed; it may be varied and superficially immense; but it escapes, for it will not reside there. Celibacy gives a restless activity to researches, intrigues, and business, a sort of huntsman's eagerness, a sharpness in the subtleties of school-divinity and disputation; this is at least the effect it had in its prime. If it makes the senses keen and liable to temptation, certainly it does not soften the heart. Our terrorists in the fifteenth and sixteenth centuries were monks.[2] Monastic prisons were always the most cruel.[3] A life systematically negative, a life without its functions, developes in man instincts that are hostile to life; he who suffers, is willing to make others suffer. The harmonious and fertile parts of our nature, which on the one hand incline to goodness, and on the other to genius and high invention, can hardly ever withstand this partial suicide.

Two classes of persons necessarily contract much insensibility— surgeons and priests. By constantly witnessing sufferings and death, we become by degrees dead in our sympathetic faculties. Let us, however, remark this difference, that the insensibility of the surgeon is not without its utility: if he was affected by his operation he might tremble. The business of the priest, on the contrary, requires that he should be affected; sympathy would be generally the most efficacious remedy to cure the soul. But independently of what we have just said about the natural harshness of this profitless life, we must observe that the priest, in contradiction with a society, the whole of whose progress he condemns, becomes less and less benevolent for the sinner and the rebel. The physician who does not like his patient is less likely than another to cure him.

It is a sad reflection to think that these men, who have so little sympathy, and who are, moreover, soured by contention, should happen to have in their hands the most gentle portion of mankind; that which has preserved the most affection, and ever remained the most faithful to nature, and which, in the very corruption of morals, is still the least corrupted by interest and hateful passions.

That is to say, that the least loving govern those who love the most.

In order to know well what use they make of this empire over women, which they claim as their own privilege, we must not confine ourselves to their flattering and wheedling ways with fashionable ladies, but inquire of the poor women whom they are able to treat unceremoniously, those especially, who, being in convents, are at the mercy of the ecclesiastical superiors, and whom they keep under lock and key, and undertake to protect alone.

We are not quite satisfied with this protection. For a long time we thought all was right; we were even simple enough to say to ourselves that the law could see nothing amiss in this kingdom of grace. But hark! from those gentle asylums, those images of paradise, we hear sobs and sighs.

I shall not speak here of the convents that have become real houses of correction, nor of the events at Sens, Avignon, and Poictiers, nor of the suicides that have taken place, alas! much nearer home.

No, I shall speak only of the most honourable houses and the most holy nuns. How are they protected by ecclesiastical authority?

First, *as to the Soul*, or conscience, that dearest possession, on account of which they sacrifice all the pleasures of this world; is it true that the sisters of the hospitals who passed for Jansenists have been latterly persecuted, to make them denounce their supposed secret directors; and that they have obtained a truce only through the threatening mediation of a magistrate, who is a celebrated orator and a firm Gallican?

Again, *as to the Body*, or personal liberty, which the slave gains as soon as ever he does but touch the sacred soil of France—does ecclesiastical authority secure this to the nuns? Is it true that a Carmelite nun, within sixty leagues of Paris, was kept *chained* for several months in her convent, and afterwards shut up for *nine years in a madhouse*?

Is it true that a Benedictine nun was put into a sort of *in pace*, and afterwards into a room full of mad women, where nothing was heard but the horrible cries, howlings, and impure language of ruined women, who, from one excess to another, have become raving mad?[4]

This woman, whose only crime was good sense and a taste for writing and drawing flowers, served her establishment a long time as housekeeper and governess: she had taught most of the sisters to read. What does she ask for? The punishment of her enemies? No: only the consolation of confessing, and taking the sacrament; spiritual food for her old age.

People may say, "Perhaps the bishop did not know?" The bishop knew all: "he was much moved"—but he did nothing. The chaplain of the house knew they were going to put a nun *in pace*. "He sighed "—but did nothing. The *Vicaire-Général* did not sigh, but sided with the party against the nun: his *ultimatum* was that she should die of hunger, or return to her dungeon.

Who showed himself the real bishop in this business?—The Magistrate. Who was the real priest? The Advocate, a studious young man, whom science had withdrawn from the bar, but who, seeing this unfortunate woman devoid of all succour, for whom no one durst either print or plead (under the ridiculous system of terror), took up the affair, spoke, wrote, and acted; taking every necessary step, making journeys in the depth of winter, and sacrificing both his money and his time—six months of his life. May God pay him back with interest!

Which is the good Samaritan in this case? Who proved himself the neighbour of the wretched woman? Who picked up the bleeding victim from the road, before whom the Pharisees had passed? Who is the real priest, the true father?

A witty writer of the day uses the term *my fathers*, in speaking of the magistrates who interpose in the affairs of the Church. He speaks deridingly, but they deserve the name. Who bestows it upon them? The afflicted who are the members of Christ, and who, as such, are also the Church, I should think. Yes, they call them *fathers* on account of their paternal equity. Their helpful interposition had too long been repelled from the threshold of the convents by these crafty words: "*What are you going to do?* Should you enter here, you would disturb the peace of these quiet asylums, and startle these timid virgins!" Why! they themselves call for our assistance: we hear their shrieks from the streets!

All of us laymen, of whatever denomination, whether magistrates, politicians, authors, or solitary thinkers, ought to take up the cause of women more seriously than we have hitherto done.

We cannot leave them where they now are, in hands so harsh and unfeeling, and which are, moreover, unsafe in more than one respect.

Nothing can be more important or more worthy of uniting us together.

Let us, I pray you, come to an understanding about it; it is the most holy of all causes: let there be then a cessation from religious strife. We can recommence our disputes afterwards as much as we please.

And first let us frankly confess the truth to one another. The evil when confessed and known has a better chance of being remedied. Whom ought we to accuse in the present state of things?

Let us not accuse the Jesuits, who carry on their Jesuitical trade, nor the priests, who are dangerous, restless, and violent, only because they are unhappy. No; we ought rather to accuse ourselves.

If dead men return in broad daylight, if these Gothic phantoms haunt our streets at noon-day, it is because the living have let the spirit of life grow weak within them. How is it that these men re-appear among us, after having been buried by history with all funeral rites, and laid by the side of other ancient orders? The very sight of them is a solemn token and a serious warning.

This has been allowed to take place, O ye men of the present day, to bring you to your senses, and to remind you of what you ought to be. If the future that is within you were revealed in its full light, who would turn his eyes towards the departing shadows of darkness and night? It is for you to find, and for you to make, the future. This is not a thing that you must expect to find ready made. If the future is already in you as a bud, transmitted from the most distant ages, let it grow there as the desire for progress and amelioration, a paternal wish for the happiness of those who are to follow you. Love in anticipation your unknown son, for he will be born. Men call him "The time to come." Then work for him.

The day when fellow-mortals will perceive in you the man of future and a magnanimous mind, families will be rallied. Woman will follow you everywhere, if she can say to herself, "I am the wife of a strong man."

Modern strength appears in the powerful liberty with which you go on disengaging the reality from the forms, and the spirit from the dead letter. But why do you not reveal yourself to the companion of your life, in that which is for you your life itself? She passes away days and years by your side, without seeing or knowing the grandeur that is within you. If she saw you walk free, strong, and prosperous in action and in science, she would not remain chained down to material idolatry, and bound to the sterile letter; she would rise to a faith far more free and pure, and you would be as one in faith. She would preserve for you this common treasure of religious life, where you might seek for comfort when your mind is languid; and when your various toils, studies, and business have weakened the vital unity within you, she would bring back your thoughts and life to God, the true, the only unity.

I shall not attempt to crowd a large volume into a small Preface. I shall only add one word, which at once expresses and completes my thought.

Man ought to nourish woman. He ought to feed spiritually (and materially if he can) her who nourishes him with her love, her milk, and her very life. Our adversaries give women bad food; but we give them none at all.

To the women of the richer class, those brilliant ones whom people suppose so happy, to these we give no spiritual food.

And to the women of the poorer class, solitary, industrious, and destitute, who try hard to gain their bread, we do not even give our assistance to help them to find their material food.

These women, who are or will be mothers, are left by us to fast (either in soul or in body), and we are punished especially by the generation that issues from them, for our neglecting to give them the staff of life.

I like to believe that good-will, generally, is not wanting—only time and attention. People live in a hurry, and can hardly be said to live: they follow with a huntsman's eagerness this or that petty object, and neglect what is important.

You man of business or study, who are so energetic and indefatigable, you have no time, say you, to associate your wife with your daily progress; you leave her to her *ennui*, idle conversations, empty sermons, and silly books; so that, falling below herself, less than woman, even less than a child, she will have neither moral action, influence, or maternal authority over her own offspring. Well! you will have the time, as old age advances, to try in vain to do all over again what is not done twice, to follow in the steps of a son, who, from college to the schools, and from thence into the world, hardly knows his family; and who, if he travels a little, and meets you on his return, will ask you your name. The mother alone could have made you a son; but to do so you ought to have made her what a woman ought to be, strengthened her with your sentiments and ideas, and nourished her with your life.

If I look beyond the family and domestic affections, I find our negligence towards women resembles hard-heartedness; the cruel effects which result from it recoil upon ourselves.

You think yourself good and kind-hearted; you are not insensible to the fate of poor women; an old one reminds you of your mother, a young one of your daughter. But you have not the time either to see or know that the old one and the young one are both literally dying with hunger.

Two machines are constantly working to exterminate them:—the convent, that immense *Workshop*, that works for little or nothing, not relying on its labour for subsistence. Then the large shop, with sleeping partners, that buys of the convent, and destroys by degrees the smaller shops which employed the workwomen. The latter has but two chances left—the Seine, or to find at night some heartless wretch who takes advantage of her hunger—suicide or dishonour.

Men receive about as much as women from public charity: this is unjust. They have infinitely more resources. They are stronger, have a greater variety of work, more *initiative*, a more active impulse, more locomotion, if I may so express myself, to go and hunt out work. They travel, emigrate, and find engagements. Not to mention countries where manual labour is very dear, I know of provinces in France, where it is very difficult to find either journeymen or man-servants. Man can wander to and fro. Woman remains at home and dies.

Let this workwoman, whom the opposition of the convent has crushed, crawl to the gate of the convent—can she find an asylum there? She would want, in default of dowry, the active protection of an influential priest, a protection reserved for devout persons, such as have had the time to follow the "*Mois de Marie*"—Devotions to the Virgin—the *Catechisms of Perseverance*, &c., &c., and who have been, for a long time past, under ecclesiastical authority. This protection is often very dearly purchased; and for what? To get permission to pass one's life shut up within walls, to be obliged to counterfeit a devotion one has not! Death cannot be worse.

They die then, quietly, decently, and alone. They will never be seen coming down from their garrets into the street to walk about with the motto, "*To live working or die fighting.*" They will make no disturbances; we have nothing to fear from them. It is for this very reason, that we are the more bound to assist them. Shall we then feel our hearts affected only for those of whom we are afraid?

Men of money, if I must speak to you in your own money language, I will tell you, that as soon as we shall have an economical government, it will not hesitate to lay out its money for women, to help them to maintain themselves by their industry.

Not only do these sickly women crowd our hospitals, and leave them only to return, but the offspring of these poor exhausted creatures, if they do not die in the Foundling, will be, like their mothers, the habitual inmates of those hospitals. A miserably poor woman is a whole family of sick persons in perspective.

Whether we be philosophers, physiologists, political economists, or statesmen, we all know that the excellency of the race, the strength of the people, come especially from the woman. Does not the nine months' support of the mother establish this? Strong mothers have strong children.

We all are, and ever shall be, the debtors of women. They are mothers; this says everything. He who would bargain about the work of those who are the joy of the present and the destiny of the future, must needs have been born in misery and damnation. Their manual labour is a very secondary consideration; that is especially our part. What do they make?—Man: this is a superior work. To be loved, to bring forth both physically and morally, to educate man (our barbarous age does not quite understand this yet), this is the business of woman.

"*Fons omnium viventium!*" What can ever be added to this sublime saying?

Whilst writing all this, I have had in my mind a woman, whose strong and serious mind would not have failed to support me in these contentions: I lost her thirty years ago (I was a child then); nevertheless, ever living in my memory, she follows me from age to age.

She suffered with me in my poverty, and was not allowed to share my better fortune. When young I made her sad, and now I cannot console her. I know not even where her bones are: I was too poor then to buy earth to bury her!

And yet I owe her much. I feel deeply that I am the son of woman. Every instant in my ideas and words (not to mention my features and gestures), I find again my mother in myself. It is my mother's blood which gives me the sympathy I feel for by-gone ages, and the tender remembrance of all those who are now no more.

What return then could I, who am myself advancing towards old age, make her for the many things I owe her? One, for which she would have thanked me—this protest in favour of women and mothers: and I place it at the head of a book believed by some to be a work of controversy. They are wrong.

The longer it lives, if it should live, the plainer will it be seen, that, in spite of polemical emotion, it was a work of history, a work of faith, of truth, and of sincerity:—on what, then, could I have set my heart more?

[1] This will not appear exaggerated to those who have read the furious libel of the Bishop of Chartres. A newspaper asks me why I did not prosecute him for defamation. This mad violence is much less guilty than the treacherous insinuations they make in their books and newspapers, in the saloons, &c. Now they attribute to me whatever has been done by other Michelets, to whom I am not even related (for instance, Michelet of Languedoc, a poet and soldier under the Restoration); now they pretend to believe, though I had told them the contrary at the end of my preface, that this book is my lecture of 1844. Then, again, they get up a little petition from Marseilles, to pray for the dismissal of the professor. So far from wishing to stifle the voice of my adversaries, I have claimed for their writings the same liberty I asked for my own. *Lesson of the 27th of February*, 1845:—"I see among you the greater part of those who had aided me to maintain in this chair the liberty of discussion. We will respect this liberty in our adversaries. This is not chivalry, it is simply our duty. It is, moreover, essential to the cause of truth, that no objection be suppressed; but that each party may be at liberty to state their reasons. You may be sure that truth will prevail and conquer. We pass away; but truth lasts and triumphs. Yet, as long as her adversaries may have any thing to say, her triumph is mingled with doubt."

[2] For the fifteenth century, see my History of France, A.D. 1413.

[3] Mabillon on *Monastic Imprisonment*, posthumous works, vol. ii. p. 327.

[4] We should, perhaps, have reserved these facts for some future occasion, if they had not been already divulged by the newspapers and reviews. Besides, several magistrates have expressed their opinions on many analogous facts in the same locality. A solicitor-general writes to the underprefect:—"I have reason to be as convinced *as you*, that Madame * * * was in full possession of her senses. A longer imprisonment would most certainly have made her really mad," &c. A letter from the Solicitor-General Sorbier, quoted by Mr. Tilliard, in favour of Marie Lemonnier, p. 65.

MEMOIR.

The following brief Memoir of the Author of "Priests, Women, and Families" was written for, and embodied in, the "Dictionary of Universal Biography," published by Mackenzie about 1862.

Another Memoir of this celebrated Historian of France was given in *The Times*, Feb. 12, 1874, two days after his decease. *The Times* states that he "died of heart disease":—

"Michelet, Jules, one of the greatest of contemporary French writers, was born at Paris on the 21st of August, 1798. In the introduction to his little book, 'Le Peuple,' Michelet has told the story of his early life. He was the son of a small master printer, of Paris, who was ruined by one of the Emperor Napoleon's arbitrary measures against the Press, by which the number of printers in Paris was suddenly reduced. For the benefit of his creditors, the elder Michelet, with no aid but that of his family, printed, folded, bound, and sold some trivial little works, of which he owned the copyright; and the Historian of France began his career by 'composing' in the typographical, not the literary, sense of the word. At twelve he had picked up a little Latin from a friendly old bookseller who had been a village schoolmaster; and his brave parents, in spite of their penury, decided that he should go to college. He entered the Lycée Charlemagne, where he distinguished himself, and his exercises attracted the notice of Villemain. He supported himself by private teaching until, in 1821, he obtained, by competition, a professorship in his college. His first publications were two chronological summaries of modern history, 1825-26. In 1827 he essayed a higher flight by the publication, not only of his 'Précis de l'Histoire Moderne,' but by that of his volume on the Scienza Nuova of Vico ('Principes de la Philosophie d'Histoire'), the then little-known father of the so-called philosophy of history, whose work was thus first introduced to the French public, and, indeed, to that of England. These two works procured him a professorship at the école normale. After the Revolution of the Three Days, the now distinguished professor was placed at the head of the historical section of the French archives, a welcome position, which gave him the command of new and unexplored material for the History of France. The first work in which he displayed his peculiar historical genius, was his 'Histoire Romaine,' 1831, embracing only the History of the Roman Republic. From 1833, dates the appearance of his great 'History of France,' of which still uncompleted work, twelve volumes had appeared in 1860. In 1834, Gruizot made the dawning Historian of France his *suppléant*, or substitute, in the Chair of History connected with the Faculty of Letters;

and in 1838 he was appointed Professor of History in the College de France. Meanwhile, besides instalments of his 'History of France,' he had published several works, among them (1835) his excellent and interesting 'Memoires de Luther,' in which, by extracts from Luther's Table-talk and Letters, the great reformer was made to tell himself the history of his life; the 'OEuvres Choises de Vico;' and the philosophical and poetical 'Origines du Droit Francais.' In the education controversy of the later years of Louis Philippe's reign, Michelet and his friend Edgar Quinet vehemently opposed the pretensions of the clerical party, and carried the war into the enemies' camp by the publication of their joint work, 'Les Jesuites,' 1843, followed, in 1844, by Michelet's 'Du Pretre, de la Femme, et la Famille,' translated into English as 'Priests, Women, and Families.' Guizot bowed to the ecclesiastical storm which these works invoked, and suspended the lectures of the two anti-clerical professors. To 1846 belongs Michelet's eloquent and touching little book, 'Le Peuple.' The Revolution of February, 1848, restored Michelet to his functions. He waived, however, the political career which was now opened to him, and laboured at his grandiose 'History of the French Revolution,' of which the first volume had appeared in 1847. In 1851 he was again suspended—this time by the ministry of the Prince President—from his professional functions, and on account of his democratic teachings. After the *coup d'etat* he refused to take the oaths, and lost all his public employments. Since then he has been occupied with his 'History of France,' and of the French Revolution, and with the production of other and some minor works. It is not among the last that must be classed his two striking volumes, 'L'Oiseau,' 1856, and 'L'Insecte,' 1857, the result of a retreat from a pressure of a new political system into the realm of nature. In 'L'Amour,' 1858, and 'La Femme,' 1859, the intrusion of physiology into the domain of thought and feeling was too much for English tastes. In 'La Mer,' 1861, Michelet addresses himself to the natural history and the poetry of the sea."

PART I.

ON DIRECTION IN THE SEVENTEENTH CENTURY.

CHAPTER I.

RELIGIOUS REACTION IN 1600.—INFLUENCE OF THE JESUITS OVER WOMEN AND CHILDREN.—SAVOY; THE VAUDOIS; VIOLENCE AND MILDNESS.—ST. FRANCOIS DE SALES.

Everybody has seen in the Louvre Guide's graceful picture representing the Annunciation. The drawing is incorrect, the colouring false, and yet the effect is seducing. Do not expect to find in it the conscientiousness and austerity of the old schools; you would look also in vain for the vigorous and bold touch of the masters of the *Renaissance*. The sixteenth century has passed away, and everything assumes a softer character. The figure with which the painter has evidently taken the most pleasure is the angel, who, according to the refinement of that surfeited period, is a pretty-looking singing boy—a cherub of the Sacristy. He appears to be sixteen, and the Virgin from eighteen to twenty years of age. This Virgin—by no means ideal, but real, and the reality slightly adulterated—is no other than a young Italian maiden whom Guido copied at her own house, in her snug oratory, and at her convenient praying-desk (prie-Dieu), such as were then used by ladies.

If the painter was inspired by anything else, it was not by the Gospel, but rather by the devout novels of that period, or the fashionable sermons uttered by the Jesuits in their coquettish-looking churches. The Angelic Salutation, the Visitation, the Annunciation, were the darling subjects upon which they had, for a long time past, exhausted every imagination of seraphic gallantry. On beholding this picture by Guide, we fancy we are reading the Bernardino. The angel speaks Latin like a young learned clerk; the Virgin, like a boarding-school young lady, responds in soft Italian, "O alto signore," &c.

This pretty picture is important as a work characteristic of an already corrupt age; being an agreeable and delicate work, we are the more easily led to perceive its suspicious graces and equivocal charms.

Let us call to mind the softened forms which the devout reaction of this age—that of Henry IV.—then assumed. We are lost in astonishment when we hear, as it were on the morrow of the sixteenth century, after wars and massacres, the lisping of this still small voice. The terrible preachers of the Sixteen,—the monks who went armed with muskets in the processions of the League—are suddenly humanised, and become gentle. The reason is, they must lull to sleep those whom they have not been able to kill. The task, however, was not very difficult. Everybody was worn out by the excessive fatigue of religious warfare, and exhausted by a struggle that afforded no result, and from which no one came off victorious. Every one knew too well his party and his friends. In the evening of so long a march there was nobody, however good a walker he might be, who did not desire to rest: the indefatigable Henry of Beam, seeking repose like the rest, or wishing to lull them into tranquillity, afforded them the example, and gave himself up with a good grace into the hands of Father Cotton and Gabrielle.

Henry IV. was the grandfather of Louis XIV., and Cotton the great uncle of Father La Chaise—two royalties, two dynasties; one of kings, the other of Jesuit confessors. The history of the latter would be very interesting. These amiable fathers ruled throughout the whole of the century, by dint of absolving, pardoning, shutting their eyes, and remaining ignorant. They effected great results by the most trifling means, such as little capitulations, secret transactions, back-doors, and hidden staircases.

The Jesuits could plead that, being the constrained restorers of Papal authority, that is to say, physicians to a dead body, the means were not left to their choice. Dead beat in the world of ideas, where could they hope to resume their warfare, save in the field of intrigue, passion, and human weaknesses?

There, nobody could serve them more actively than Women. Even when they did not act with the Jesuits and for them, they were not less useful in an indirect manner, as instruments and means,—as objects of business and daily compromise between the penitent and the confessor.

The tactics of the confessor did not differ much from those of the mistress. His address, like hers, was to refuse sometimes, to put off, to cause to languish, to be severe, but with moderation, then at length to be overcome by pure goodness of heart. These little manoeuvres, infallible in their effects upon a gallant and devout king, who was moreover obliged to receive the sacrament on appointed days, often put the whole State into the Confessional. The king being caught and held fast, was obliged to give satisfaction in some way or other. He paid for his human weaknesses with political ones; such an amour cost him a state-secret, such a bastard a royal ordinance. Occasionally, they did not let him off without bail. In order to preserve a certain mistress, for instance, he was forced to give up his son. How much did Father Cotton forgive Henry IV. to obtain from him the education of the dauphin.[1]

In this great enterprise of kidnapping man everywhere, by using woman as a decoy, and by woman getting possession of the child, the

Jesuits met with more than one obstacle, but one particularly serious—their reputation of Jesuits. They were already by far too well known. We may read in the letters of St. Charles Borromeo, who had established them at Milan and {36} singularly favoured them, what sort of character he gives them—intriguing, quarrelsome, and insolent under a cringing exterior. Even their penitents, who found them very convenient, were nevertheless at times disgusted with them. The most simple saw plainly enough that these people, who found every opinion probable, had none themselves. These famous champions of the faith were sceptics in morals: even less than sceptics, for speculative scepticism might leave some sentiment of honour; but a doubter in practice, who says Yes on such and such an act, and Yes on the contrary one, must sink lower and lower in morality, and lose not only every principle, but in time every affection of the heart!

Their very appearance was a satire against them. These people, so cunning in disguising themselves, were made up of lying; it was everywhere around them, palpable and visible. Like brass badly gilt, like the holy toys in their gaudy churches, they appeared false at the distance of a hundred paces: false in expression, accent, gesture, and attitude; affected, exaggerated, and often excessively fickle. This inconstancy was amusing, but it also put people on their guard. They could well learn an attitude or a deportment; but studied graces, and a bending, undulating, and serpentine gait are anything but satisfactory. They worked hard to appear a simple, humble, insignificant, good sort of people. Their grimace betrayed them.

These equivocal-looking individuals had, however, in the eyes of the women a redeeming quality: they were passionately fond of children. No mother, grandmother, or nurse could caress them more, or could find better some endearing word to make them smile. In the churches of the Jesuits the good saints of the order, St. Xavier or St. Ignatius, are often painted as grotesque nurses, holding the divine darling (poupon) in their arms, fondling and kissing it. They began also to make on their altars and in their fantastically-ornamented chapels those little paradises in glass cases, where women are delighted to see the wax child among flowers. The Jesuits loved children so much, that they would have liked to educate them all.

Not one of them, however learned he might be, disdained to be a tutor, to give the principles of grammar, and teach the declensions.

There were, however, many people among their own friends and penitents, even those who trusted their souls to their keeping, who, nevertheless, hesitated to confide their sons to them. They would have succeeded far less with women and children, if their good fortune had not given them for ally a tall lad, shrewd and discreet, who possessed precisely what they had lacked to inspire confidence,—a charming simplicity.

This friend of the Jesuits, who served them so much the better as he did not become one of them, invented, in an artless manner, for the profit of these intriguers, the manner, tone, and true style of easy devotion, which they would have ever sought for in vain. Falsehood would never assume the shadow of reality as it can do, if it was always and entirely unconnected with truth.

Before speaking of François de Sales, I must say one word about the stage on which he performs his part.

The great effort of the Ultramontane reaction about the year 1600 was at the Alps, in Switzerland and Savoy. The work was going on bravely on each side of the mountains, only the means were far from being the same: they showed on either side a totally different countenance—here the face of an angel, there the look of a wild beast; the latter physiognomy was against the poor Vaudois in Piedmont.

In Savoy, and towards Geneva, they put on the angelic expression, not being able to employ any other than gentle means against populations sheltered by treaties, and who would have been protected against violence by the lances of Switzerland.

The agent of Rome in this quarter was the celebrated Jesuit, Antonio Possevino[2], a professor, scholar, and diplomatist, as {38} well as the confessor of the kings of the North. He himself organised the persecutions against the Vaudois of Piedmont; and he formed and directed his pupil, François de Sales, to gain by his address the Protestants of Savoy.

Ought I to speak of this terrible history of the Vaudois, or pass it over in silence? Speak of it! It is far too cruel—no one will relate it without his pen hesitating, and his words being blotted by his tears.[3] If, however, I did not speak of it, we should never behold the most odious part of the system, that artful policy which employed the very opposite means in precisely the same cases; here ferocity, there an unnatural mildness. One word, and I leave the sad story. The most implacable butchers were women, the penitents of the Jesuits of Turin. The victims were children! They destroyed them in the sixteenth century: there were four hundred children burnt at one time in a cavern. In the seventeenth century they kidnapped them. The edict of pacification, granted to the Vaudois in 1655, promises, as a singular favour, that their children under twelve years of age shall no longer be stolen from them; above that age it is still lawful to seize them.

This new sort of persecution, more cruel than massacres, characterises the period when the Jesuits undertook to make themselves universally masters of the education of children. These pitiless plagiarists[4], who dragged them away from their mothers, wanted only to bring them up in their fashion, make them abjure their faith, hate their family, and arm them against their brethren.

It was, as I have said, a Jesuit professor, Possevino, who renewed the persecution about the time at which we are now arrived. The same, while teaching at Padua, had for his pupil young François de Sales, who had already passed a year in Paris, at the college of Clermont. He belonged to one of those families of Savoy, as much distinguished by their devotion as by their valour, who carried on wars long against Geneva. He was endowed with all the qualities requisite for the war of seduction, which they then desired to commence—a gentle and sincere devotion, a lively and earnest speech, and a singular charm of goodness, beauty, and gentleness. Who has not remarked this charm in the smile of the children of Savoy, who are so natural, yet so circumspect?

Every favour of Heaven must, we certainly believe, have been showered upon him, since in this bad age, bad taste, and bad party, among the cunning and false people who made him their tool, he remained, however, St. François de Sales. Everything he has said or written, without being free from blemishes, is charming, full of affection, of an original gentleness and genius, which, though it may excite a smile, is nevertheless very affecting. Everywhere we find, as it were, living fountains springing up, flowers after flowers, and rivulets meandering as in a lovely spring morning after a shower. It might be said, perhaps, that he amuses himself so much with flowerets, that his nosegay is no longer such as shepherdesses gather, but such as would suit a flower-girl, as his Philothea would say: he takes them all, and takes too many; there are some colours among them badly matched, and have a strange effect. It is the taste of that age, we must confess; the Savoyard taste in particular does not fear ugliness; and a Jesuit education does not lead to the detestation of falsehood.

But even if he had not been so charming a writer, his bewitching personal qualities would still have had the same effect. His fair mild countenance, with rather a childish expression, pleased at first sight. Little children, in their nurses' arms, as soon as they saw him, could not take their eyes off him. He was equally delighted with them, and would exclaim, as he fondly caressed them, "Here is my little family." The children ran after him, and the mothers followed their children.

Little family? or little intrigue? The words (*ménage manège*) are somewhat similar; and though a child in appearance, the good man was at bottom very deep. If he permitted the nuns a few trifling falsehoods[5], ought we to believe he never granted the same indulgence to himself? However it may be, actual falsehood appeared less in his words than in his position; he was made a bishop in order to give the example of sacrificing the rights of the bishops to the Pope. For the love of peace, and to hide the division of the Catholics by an appearance of union, he did the Jesuits the important service of saving their Molina accused at Rome; and he managed to induce the Pope to impose silence on the friends, as well as the enemies, of Grace.

This sweet-tempered man did not, however, confine himself to the means of mildness and persuasion. In his zeal as a converter, he invoked the assistance of less honourable means—interest, money, places; lastly, authority and terror. He made the Duke of Savoy travel from village to village, and advised him at last to drive away the remaining few who still refused to abjure their faith.[6] Money, very powerful in this poor country, seemed to him a means at once so natural and irresistible, that he went even into Geneva, to buy up old Theodore de Bèze, and offered him, on the part of the Pope, a pension of four thousand crowns.

It was an odd sight to behold this man, the bishop and titular prince of Geneva, beating about the bush to circumvent his native city, and organising a war of seduction against it by France and Savoy. Money and intrigue did not suffice; it was necessary to employ a softer charm to thaw and liquify the inattackable iceberg of logic and criticism. Convents for females were founded, to attract and receive the newly-converted, and to offer them a powerful bait composed of love and mysticism. These convents have been made famous by the names of Madame de Chantal and Madame Guyon. The former established in them the mild devotion of the Visitation; and it was there that the latter wrote her little book of *Torrents*, which seems inspired, like Rousseau's *Julie* (by the bye, a far less dangerous composition), by the Charmettes, Meillerie, and Clarens.

[1] The masterpiece of the Jesuit was to get the shepherd-poet Des Yveteaux, the most empty-headed man in France, named tutor, reserving to himself the moral and religious part of education.

[2] See his Life, by Dorigny, p. 505.; Bonneville, Life of St. François, p. 19, &c.

[3] Read the three great Vaudois historians, Gilles, Léger, and Arnaud.

[4] Plagiarius, in its proper sense, means, as is well known, a man-stealer.

[5] Little lies, little deceits, little prevarications. See, for instance, OEuvres, vol. viii. pp. 196, 223, 342.

[6] Nouvelles Lettres Inédites, published by Mr. Datta, 1835, vol. i. p. 247. See also, for the intolerance of St. François, pp. 130, 131, 136, 141, and vol. ix. of the OEuvres, p. 335, the bounden duty of kings to put to the sword all the enemies of the Pope.

CHAPTER II.

Saint François de Sales was very popular in France, and especially in the provinces of Burgundy, where a fermentation of religious passions had continued in full force ever since the days of the League. The parliament of Dijon entreated him to come and preach there. He was received by his friend André Frémiot, who from being a counsellor in Parliament had become Archbishop of Bourges. He was the son of a president much esteemed at Dijon, and the brother of Madame de Chantal, consequently the great-uncle of Madame de Sévigné, who was the grand-daughter of the latter.

The biographers of St. François and Madame de Chantal, in order to give their first meeting an air of the romantic and marvellous, suppose, but with little probability on their side, that they were unacquainted; that one had scarcely heard the other spoken of; that they had seen each other only in their dreams or visions. In Lent, when the Saint preached at Dijon, he distinguished her among the crowd of ladies, and, on descending from the pulpit, exclaimed, "Who is then this young widow, who listened so attentively to the Word of God?" "My sister," replied the Archbishop, "the Baroness de Chantal."

She was then (1604) thirty-two years of age, and St. Francis thirty-seven; consequently, she was born in 1572, the year of St. Bartholomew. From her very infancy she was somewhat austere, passionate, and violent. When only six years old, a Protestant gentleman happening to give her some sugar-plums, she threw them into the fire, saying, "Sir, see how the heretics will burn in hell, for not believing what our Lord has said. If you gave the lie to the king, my papa would have you hung; what must the punishment be then for having so often contradicted our Lord!"

With all her devotion and passion, she had an eye to real advantages. She had very ably conducted the household and fortune of her husband, and those of her father and father-in-law were managed by her with the same prudence. She took up her abode with the latter, who, otherwise, had not left his wealth to her young children.

We read with a sort of enchantment the lively and charming letters by which the correspondence begins between St. François de Sales, and her whom he calls "his dear sister and daughter." Nothing can be more pure and chaste, but at the same time, why should we not say so, nothing more ardent. It is curious to observe the innocent art, the caresses, the tender and ingenious flattery with which he envelopes these two families, the Frémiots and the Chantals. First, the father, the good old president Frémiot, who in his library begins to study religious books and dreams of salvation; next, the brother, the ex-chancellor, the Archbishop of Bourges; he writes expressly for him a little treatise on the manner of preaching. He by no means neglects the father-in-law, the rough old Baron de Chantal, an ancient relic of the wars of the League, the object of the daughter-in-law's particular adoration. But he succeeds especially in captivating the young children; he shows his tenderness in a thousand ways, by a thousand pious caresses, such as the heart of a woman, and that woman a mother, had scarcely been able to suggest. He prays for them, and desires these infants to remember him in their prayers.

Only one person in this household was difficult to be tamed, and this was Madame de Chantal's confessor. It is here, in this struggle between the Director and the Confessor, that we learn what address, what skilful manoeuvres and stratagems, are to be found in the resources of an ardent will. This confessor was a devout personage, but of confined and shallow intellect, and small means. The Saint desires to become his friend,—he submits to his superior wisdom the advice he is about to give. He skilfully comforts Madame de Chantal, who entertained some misgiving about her spiritual infidelity, and who, finding herself moving on an agreeable sloping path, was fearful she had left the rough road to salvation. He carefully entertains this scruple in order the better to do away with it; to her inquiry whether she ought to impart it to her confessor, he adroitly gives her to understand that it may be dispensed with.

He declares then as a conqueror, who has nothing to fear, that far from being, like the other, uneasy, jealous, and peevish, who required implicit obedience, he on the contrary imposes no obligations, but leaves her entirely free—no obligation, save that of Christian friendship, whose tie is called by St. Paul "the bond of perfectness:" all other ties are temporal, even that of obedience; but that of charity increases with time: it is free from the scythe of death,—"Love is strong as death," saith the Song of Solomon. He says to her, on another occasion, with much ingenuousness and dignity: "I do not add one grain to the truth; I speak before God, who knows my heart and yours; every affection has a character that distinguishes it from the others; that which I feel for you has a peculiar character, that gives me infinite consolation, and to tell you all, is extremely profitable to me. I did not wish to say so much, but one word produces another, and then I know you will be careful." (Oct. 14, 1604.)

From this moment, having her constantly before his eyes, he associates her not only with his religious thoughts, but, what astonishes us more, with his very acts as a priest. It is generally before or after mass that he writes to her; it is of her, of her children, that he is thinking, says he, "*at the moment of the communion.*" They do penance the same days, take the communion at the same moment, though separate. "*He offers her to God, when he offers Him His Son!*" (Nov. 1, 1605.)

This singular man, whose serenity was never for a moment affected by such a union, was able very soon to perceive that the mind of Madame de Chantal was far from being as tranquil as his own. Her character was strong, and she felt deeply. The middle class of people, the citizens and lawyers, from whom she was descended, were endowed from their birth with a keener mind, and a greater spirit of sincerity and truth, than the elegant, noble, but enfeebled families of the sixteenth century. The last comers were fresh; you find them everywhere ardent and serious in literature, warfare, and religion; they impart to the seventeenth century the gravity and holiness of its character. Thus this woman, though a saint, had nevertheless depths of unknown passion.

They had hardly been separated two months when she wrote to him that she wanted to see him again. And indeed they met half-way in Franche-Comte, in the celebrated pilgrimage of St. Claude. There she was happy; there she poured out all her heart, and confessed to him for the first time; making him the sweet engagement of entrusting to his beloved hand the vow of obedience.

Six weeks had not passed away before she wrote to him that she wanted to see him again. Now she is bewildered by passions and temptations; all around her is darkness and doubts; she doubts even of her faith; she has no longer the strength of exercising her will; she would wish to fly—alas! she has no wings; and in the midst of these great but sad feelings, this serious person seems rather childish; she would like him to call her no longer "madam," but his sister, his daughter, as he did before.

She uses in another place this sad expression,—"There is something within me that has never been satisfied."—(Nov. 21, 1604.)

The conduct of St. François deserves our attention. This man, so shrewd at other times, will now understand but half. Far from inducing Madame de Chantal to adopt a religious life, which would have put her into his power, he tries to strengthen her in her duties of mother and daughter towards her children and the two old men who required also her maternal care. He discourses with her of her duties, business, and obligations. As to her doubts, she must neither reflect nor reason about them. She must occasionally read good books; and he points out to her, as such, some paltry mystic treatises. If the *she-ass* should kick (it is thus he designates the flesh and sensuality), he must quiet her by some blows of discipline.

He appears at this time to have been very sensible that an intimacy between two persons so united by affection was not without inconvenience. He answers with prudence to the entreaties of Madame de Chantal: "I am bound here hand and foot; and as for you, my dear sister, does not the inconvenience of the last journey alarm you?"

This was written in October on the eve of a season rude enough among the Alps and at Jura: "We shall see between this and Easter."

She went at this period to see him at the house of his mother; then, finding herself all alone at Dijon, she fell very ill. Occupied with the controversy of this time, he seemed to be neglecting her. He wrote to her less and less; feeling, doubtless, the necessity of making all haste in this rapid journey. All this year (1605) was passed, on her part, in a violent struggle between temptations and doubts; at last she scarcely knew how to make up her mind, whether to bury herself with the Carmelites, or marry again.

A great religious movement was then taking place in France: this movement, far from being spontaneous, was well devised, very artificial, but, nevertheless, immense in its results. The rich and powerful families of the Bar had, by their zeal and vanity, impelled it forward. At the side of the oratory founded by Cardinal de Bérulle, Madame Acarie, a woman singularly active and zealous, a saint engaged in all the devout intrigues (known also as the blessed Mary of the incarnation), established the Carmelites in France, and the Ursulines in Paris. The impassioned austerity of Madame de Chantal urged her towards the Carmelites; she consulted occasionally one of their superiors, a doctor of the Sorbonne.[1] St. François de Sales perceived the danger, and he no longer endeavoured to contend against her. He accepted Madame de Chantal from that very moment. In a charming letter he gives her, in the name of his mother, his young sister to educate.

It seems that as long as she had this tender pledge she was in some degree calmer; but it was soon taken from her. This child, so cherished and so well taken care of, died in her arms at her own house. She cannot disguise from the Saint, in the excess of her grief, that she had asked God to let her rather die herself; she went so far as to pray that she might rather lose one of her own children!

This took place in November (1607). It is three months after that we find in the letters of the Saint the first idea of getting nearer to him a person so well tried, and who seemed to him, moreover, to be an instrument of the designs of God.

The extreme vivacity, I was almost saying the violence, with which Madame de Chantal broke every tie in order to follow an impulse given with so much reserve, proves too plainly all the passion of her ardent nature. It was not an easy thing to leave there those two old men, her father, her father-in-law, and her own son, who, they say, stretched himself out on the threshold to prevent her passing. Good old Frémiot was gained over less by his daughter than by the letters of the Saint, which she used as auxiliaries. We have still the letter of resignation, all blotted over with his tears, in which he gives his consent: this resignation, moreover, seems not to have lasted long. He died the following year.

She has now passed over the body of her son and that of her father; she arrives at Annecy. What would have happened if the Saint had not found fuel for this powerful flame that he had raised too high—higher than he desired himself?

The day after the Pentecost, he calls her to him after mass: "Well, my daughter," says he, "I have determined what I shall do with you." "And I am resolved to obey," cried she, falling on her knees before him. "You must enter St. Clair's." "I am quite ready," replied she. "No, you are not strong enough; you must be a sister in the Hospital of Beaune." "Whatever you please." "This is not quite what I want—become a Carmelite." He tried her thus in several ways, and found her ever obedient. "Well," said he, "nothing of the sort—God calls you to the Visitation."

The Visitation had nothing of the austerity of the ancient orders. The founder himself said it was "almost no religion at all." No troublesome customs, no watchings, no fastings, but little duty, short prayers, no seclusions (in the beginning); the sisters, while they waited for the coming of the divine Bridegroom, went to visit Him in the person of His poor and His sick, who are His living members. Nothing was better calculated to calm the stormy passions within, than this variety of active charity. Madame de Chantal, who had formerly been a good mother, a prudent housekeeper, was happy in finding even in mystic life employment for her economical and positive faculties in devoting herself to the laborious detail of the establishment of a great order, in travelling, according to the orders of her beloved director, from one establishment to another. It was a twofold proof of wisdom in the Saint: he made her useful, and kept her away.

With all this prudence, we must say that the happiness of working together for the same end, of founding, and creating together, strengthened still more the tie that was already so strong. It is curious to see how they tighten the band in wishing to untie it. This contradiction is affecting. At the very time he is prescribing to her to detach herself from him who had been her nurse, he protests that this nurse shall never fail her. The very day he lost his mother he writes in these strong terms: "To you I speak, to you, I say, to whom I have allotted my mother's place in my memorial of the mass, without depriving you of the one you had, for I have not been able to do it, so fast do you retain what you have in my heart; and so it is, *you possess it first and last.*"

I do not think a stronger expression ever escaped the heart on a more solemn day. How burning must it have entered her heart, already lacerated with passion! How can he be surprised after that, that she should write to him, "Pray to God, that I survive you not!" Does he not see, that at every instant he wounds, and heals only to renew the pain?

The nuns of the Visitation, who published some of the letters of their foundress, have prudently suppressed several, which, as they say themselves, "are only fit to be kept under the lock and key of charity." Those which are extant are, however, quite sufficient to show the deep wound she bore with her to the grave.

The Visitation being supported neither by active charity, which was soon prohibited, nor by the cultivation of the intellect, which had given life to the Paraclet and other convents of the middle ages, had no other choice, it would seem, than to adopt mystic asceticism. But the moderation of the founder, in conformity with the lukewarmness of the times, had excluded from his new institution the austerity of the ancient orders—those cruel practices that annihilated the senses in destroying the body itself; consequently, there was no activity, nor study, nor austerity. In this vacuum two things were evident from the very outset: on one side, narrow-mindedness, a taste for trivial observances, and a fantastical system of devotion (Madame de Chantal tatooed her bosom with the name of Jesus); on the other side, an unreasonable and boundless attachment to the *Director.*

In everything relating to St. François de Sales the saint shows herself very weak. After his death she raves, and allows herself to be guided by dreams and visions. She fancies that she perceives his dear presence, in the churches, amid celestial perfumes, perceptible to her alone. She lays upon his tomb a little book composed of all he had written or said upon the Visitation, praying "that if there was anything in it contrary to his intentions, he would have the goodness to efface it."

In 1631, ten years after the death of St. François de Sales, his tomb was solemnly opened, and his body was found entire. "It was placed in the sacristy of the monastery, where, about nine o'clock at night, after the crowd had withdrawn, she led her community, and began praying by the side of the body, 'in an ecstasy of love and humility.' As they were forbidden to touch it, she did a signal act of obedience in abstaining from kissing his hand. The following morning, having obtained permission, she stooped down in order to place the saint's hand upon her head; when, as if he had been alive, he drew her towards him, and held her in a paternal and tender caress: she felt very plainly this supernatural movement.... They still keep, as a double relic, the veil she then wore."

Let others be at a loss to find out the real name of this worthy sentiment, or let a false reserve prevent them; let them term it filial piety, or fraternal affection; we, for our part, call it simply by a name that we believe holy—we shall call it love. We are bound to believe the saint himself, when he assures us that this sentiment contributed powerfully to his spiritual progress. However, this is not sufficient; we must see what effect it had upon Madame de Chantal.

All the doctrine to be found in the writings of St. François, among much excellent practical advice, might be summed up in these words—to *love* and to *wait*.

To wait for the visitation of the divine Bridegroom. Far from advising action, or the desire of acting, he is so afraid of motion, that he proscribes the word *union* with God, which might imply a tendency to unite; and desires that the word *unity* may be used instead, for it is necessary to remain in a loving indifference. "I wish for very little," said he, "and that little I desire very little; I have almost no desires; but if I were to be born again, I would have none at all. If God came to me, I would go to Him also; but *if He would not come to me, I would remain there, and not go to Him.*"

This absence of every desire excluded even that of virtue. It is the highest point which the saint seems to have reached a short time before his death. He writes on the 10th of August, 1619, "Say you renounce every virtue, desiring them only as you receive them gradually from God, nor wishing to take any care for acquiring them, excepting in proportion as His bounty shall employ you to do so, for His own good pleasure." If self-will disappear at this point, what will take its place? The will of God apparently.... Only, let us not forget that if this miracle take place, it will have for its result a state of unalterable peace and immutable strength. By this token, and by no other, are we bound to recognise it.

Madame de Chantal herself tells us that it had just the contrary effect. Though they have skilfully arranged her life, and mutilated her letters, there are still enough of them to show in what a tempest of passion she passed her days. Her whole life, which was long, and taken up with real cares, in founding and managing religious establishments, contributes in no way to calm her; time wears her out and destroys her, without effecting any change in her inward martyrdom. She finishes by this confession in her latter days: "All that I have suffered during the whole course of my life are not to be compared to the torments I now feel; I am reduced to such a degree that nothing can satisfy me, nor give me any relief, except one word—Death!"

I did not need this sad testimony; I could have found it out without her assistance. This exclusive cultivation of sensibility, whatever be the virtues that ennoble it, ends infallibly in tormenting the soul, and reducing it to a state of excruciating suffering. We cannot, with impunity, allow our will, the very essence of our strength and reason, the guardian of our tranquillity, to be absorbed by an all-devouring love.

I have spoken elsewhere of the few but splendid examples exhibited throughout the middle ages in the persons of learned nuns, who combined science with piety. Their instructors seem to have entertained no apprehension in developing both their reason and their will. But science, it is said, fills the soul with uneasiness and curiosity, and removes us from God. As if there were any science without Him; as if the divine effulgence, reflected in science, had not a serene virtue, a power diffusing tranquillity in the human heart, and imparting that peace of eternal truths and imperishable laws, which will exist in all their purity when worlds will be no more.

Whom do I blame in all this? Man? God forbid! I only censure the method.

This method, which was termed Quietism when once it was reduced to a system, and which, as we shall see presently, is, generally speaking, that of the *devout direction*, is nothing else than the development of our passiveness, our instinct of indolence; the result of which, in course of time, is the paralysis of our will, the annihilation of the essence of man's constitution.

St. François de Sales, was, it would seem, one of the most likely persons to impart animation to this lifeless system. Nevertheless it was he, the loyal and the pure, who introduced the system at this period; it was he who in the seventeenth century pointed out the road to *passiveness*.

We are, as yet, in the earliest dawn of the century, in all its morning freshness, and invigorated by the breeze from the Alps. Yet see, Madame de Chantal sickens and breathes with difficulty.... How will it be towards evening?

The worthy saint, in a delightful letter, describes himself as being one day on the lake of Geneva, "on a small raft," guided by Providence, and perfectly obedient "to the pilot, who forbids him to stir, and very glad at having only a board three fingers thick to support him." The century is embarked with him, and, with this amiable guide, he sails among breakers. These deep waters, as you will find out afterwards, are the depths of Quietism; and if your sight is keen enough, you may already perceive Molinos through this transparent abyss.

[1] See St. François, OEuvres, viii. 336, April, 1606; and Tabaraud, Life of Bérulle, pp., 57, 58, 95, 141.

CHAPTER III.

Hitherto we have spoken of a rare exception—the life of a woman full of action, and doubly employed; as a saint and foundress, but especially as a wife, the mother of a family, and prudent housewife. The biographers of Madame de Chantal remark, as a singular thing, that in both conditions, as wife and as widow, she conducted her own household herself, directed her dependents, and administered the property of her husband, her father, and her children.

This indeed was becoming rare. The taste for household and domestic cares which we find everywhere in the sixteenth century, but especially among citizens and the families of the Bar, grows much weaker in the seventeenth, when every one desires to live in great style.

The absence of occupation is a taste of the period, proceeding also from the state of things. All society is ever idle on the morrow of religious wars, each local action has ceased, and central life, that is to say, court life, has hardly begun. The nobility have finished their adventures, and hung up their swords; the citizens have nothing further to do, being no longer engaged in plots, seditions, or armed processions. The *ennui* of this want of occupation falls particularly heavy upon woman; she is about to become at once unoccupied and lonely. In the sixteenth century she was kept in communication with man by the vital questions that were debated, even in her family, by common dangers, fears, and hopes. But there was nothing of the sort in the seventeenth century.

Add to this a more serious circumstance which is likely to increase in the following ages; namely, that in every profession the spirit of speciality and detail, which gradually absorbs man, has the effect of insulating him in his family, and of making him, as it were, a mute being for his wife and kindred. He no longer communicates to them his daily thoughts; and they can understand nothing of the minute intricacies and petty technical problems which occupy his mind.

But, at least, woman has still her children to console her? No; at the time we are now speaking of, the mansion, silent and empty, is no longer kept alive by the noise of children; instruction at home is now an exception, and gives way daily to the fashion of collective education. The son is brought up among the Jesuits, the daughter by the Ursulines, or other nuns; the mother is left alone.

The mother and the son are henceforth separated! An immense evil, the bud of a thousand misfortunes for families and society! I shall return to this subject later.

Not only separated, but, by the effect of a totally opposite life, they will be more and more opposed in mind, and less and less able to understand each other. The son a little pedant in *us*, *i.e.* Latin, the mother ignorant and worldly, have no longer a common language between them.

A family thus disunited will be much more open to influence from without. The mother and the child, once separated, are more easily caught; though different means are employed. The child is tamed, and broken in by an overwhelming mass of studies; he must write and write, copy and copy again, at best translate and imitate. But the mother is entrapped by means of her excessive loneliness and *ennui*. The lady of the mansion is alone in her residence; her husband is hunting, or at the court. The president's lady is alone in her hotel; the gentleman starts every morning for the palace, and returns in the evening: a sad abode is this hotel in the Marais or City, some overgrown grey house in a dismal little street.

The lady in the sixteenth century beguiled her leisure hours by singing, and often by poetry. In the seventeenth they forbad her all worldly songs; as to religious songs, she abstains from them much more easily. Sing a psalm! It would be to declare herself a Protestant! What then remains for her? Gallant devotion—the conversation of the director or the lover.

The sixteenth century, with its strong morality and fluctuation of ideas, took, as it were, by fits and starts, flying leaps from gallantry to devotion, then from God to the devil: it made sudden and alternate changes from pleasure to penitence. But in the seventeenth century people were more ingenious. Thanks to the progress of equivocation, they are enabled to do both at once, and, by mingling the language of love with that of devotion, speak of both at the same time. If, without being seen, you could listen to the conversation in a coquettish neighbourhood, you would not always be able to say whether it is the lover or the director who is speaking.

To explain to one's self the singular success of the latter, we must not forget the moral situation of the time, the uneasy and bewildered state of every one's conscience on the morrow of a period of religious wars, harassed by passions. In the dull tranquillity that succeeded, in the nullity of the present, the past would rise up in glowing colours, and the remembrance of it become the more importunate. Then was awakened in many minds, especially among weak and impassioned women, the terrible question of eternal bliss or woe.

The whole fortune of the Jesuits, and the confidence placed in them by the nobles and fine ladies, arose from the clever answer they gave to this question. It is, therefore, indispensable to say a few words about it.

Who can save us? The theologian on the one hand, and the jurist or philosopher on the other, give diametrically opposite answers.

The theologian, if he be really such, attributes the greatest share to Christianity, and answers, "It is the grace of Christ, which serves us as a substitute for justice[1], and saves whomsoever it will. A few are predestined to be saved, the greater number to be damned."

The jurist answers, on the contrary, that we are punished or rewarded according to the good or bad use that we freely make of our will; that we are paid according to our works, according to justice. This is the eternal debate between the jurist and the theologian, between justice and predestination.[1]

In order to have a clearer idea of the opposition of these two principles, let us imagine a mountain with two declivities, its summit terminating in a very narrow ridge, with the edge as sharp as a razor. On one side is predestination that damns, on the other, justice that strikes— two terrible monsters. Man is on the top, with one foot on one slope and one on the other, ever on the point of slipping.

And when was the fear of sliding stronger than after those great crimes of the sixteenth century, when Man was top-heavy, and lost his balance? We know the religious horror of Charles IX. after the massacre of Saint Bartholomew: he died for want of a Jesuit confessor. John III., King of Sweden, who killed his brother, did not die of remorse: his wife took care to send for the good Father Possevino, who purified him and made him a Catholic.

The means employed by the Jesuits to calm consciences fill us, at first sight, with surprise. They adopted both skilfully and carefully; still they did adopt the principle of the jurists, namely, that man is saved or lost by his works, by the use he makes of his free will.

A liberal doctrine, yet severe, it would seem: you are free, consequently responsible, and punishable. You sin, and you expiate.

The jurisconsult, who is in earnest, requires here a serious expiation—the personal chastisement of the guilty party. "He must forfeit his head," says he: "the law will cure him of his malady of iniquity by the sword."

We should fare better by going to the Jesuit, and get off much cheaper. The expiation he requires is not so terrible. He will often prove that there is no necessity for any expiation. The fault, properly interpreted, will turn out, perhaps, to be a merit. At the worst, if found to be a fault, it may be washed out by good works; now, the very best work of all is to devote one's self to the Jesuits, and espouse the Ultramontane interest.

Do you perceive all the skill of the Jesuits in this manoeuvre of theirs? On the one hand, the doctrine of liberty and justice, with which the middle ages had reproached the jurisconsults as pagan and irreconcilable with Christianity, is now adopted by the Jesuits, who show themselves to the world as the friends and champions of free will. On the other hand, as this free will brings on the sinner responsibility and justice according to his works, he finds himself very much embarrassed with it. The Jesuit comes very seasonably to his relief; he takes upon himself the task of *directing* this inconvenient liberty, and reduces works to the capital one of serving Rome. So that moral liberty, professed in theory, will turn practically to the profit of authority.

A double lie. These people who give themselves the title of Jesuits, or men of Jesus, teach that man is saved less by Jesus than by himself, by his free will. Are, then, these men philosophers, and friends of liberty? Quite the contrary; they are at once the most cruel enemies of philosophy and liberty.

That is to say, with the word free will they juggle away Jesus; and only retain the word Jesus to cheat us of the liberty which they set before us.

The thing being thus simplified on both sides, a sort of tacit bargain was made between Rome, the Jesuits, and the world.

Rome gave up *Christianity*, the principle which forms its basis (salvation by Christ). Having been called upon to choose between this doctrine and the contrary one, she durst not decide.

The Jesuits gave up *morality* after religion; reducing the moral merits by which man may earn his salvation to only one, the *Political* merit of which we have spoken, that of serving Rome.

What must the world give up in its turn?

The world (by far the most worldly part of the world, woman) will have to give up her best possessions, her family and her domestic hearth.

Eve once more betrays Adam. Woman deceives man in her husband and son.

Thus every one sold his God. Rome bartered away religion, and woman domestic piety.

The weak minds of women after the great corruption of the sixteenth century, spoiled beyond all remedy, full of passion, fear, and wicked desires mingled with remorse, seized greedily the means of sinning conscientiously, of expiating without either amendment, amelioration, or return towards God. They thought themselves happy to receive at the Confessional, by way of penance, some little political commission, or the management of some intrigue. They transferred to this singular manner of expiating their faults the very violence of the guilty passions, for which the atonement was to be made; and in order to remain sinful, they were often obliged to commit crimes.[2]

The passion of woman, inconstant in everything else, was in this case sustained by the vigorous obstinacy of the mysterious and invisible hand that urged her forward. Under this impulse, at once gentle and strong, ardent and persevering, firm as iron and as dissolving as fire, characters and even interests at length gave way.

Some examples will help us to understand it the better. In France, old Lesdiguières was politically, much interested in remaining a Protestant; as such, he was the head man of the party. The king rather than the governor of Dauphiné, he assisted the Swiss, and protected the populations of Vaud and Romand against the house of Savoy. But the old man's daughter was gained over by Father Cotton. She set to work upon her father with patience and address, and succeeded in inducing him to quit his high position for an empty title, and change his religion for the title of Constable.

In Germany the character of Ferdinand I., his interest, and the part he had to play, would have induced him to remain moderate, and not become the vassal of his nephew, Philip II. With violence and fanaticism he had no choice but to accept a secondary place. The emperor's daughters, however, intrigued so well that the house of Austria became united by marriage to the houses of Lorraine and Bavaria. The children of these families being educated by the Jesuits, the latter repaired in Germany the broken thread of the destinies of the Guises, and had even better fortune than the Guises themselves; for they made for their own use certain blind instruments, agents in diplomacy and tactics—skilful workmen certainly, but still mere workmen. I speak of that hardy and devout generation, of Ferdinand II. of Austria, of Tilly, and Maximilian of Bavaria, those conscientious executors of the great works of Rome, who, under the direction of their teachers, carried on for so long a time, throughout Europe, a warfare which was at once barbarous and skilful, merciless and methodical. The Jesuits launched them into it, and then carefully watched over them; and whenever Tilly on his charger was seen dashing over the smoking ruins of cities, or the battle-field covered with the slain, the Jesuit, trotting on his mule, was not far off.

This vile war, the most loathsome in history, appears the more horrible, by the almost total absence of free inspiration and spontaneous impulse. It was, from its very beginning, both artificial and mechanical[3]— like a war of machines or phantoms. These strange beings, created only to fight, march with a look as void of martial ardour, as their heart is of affection. How could they be reasoned with? What language could be used towards them? What pity could be expected from them? In our wars of religion, in those of the Revolution they were men who fought; each died for the sake of his idea, and, when he fell on the battle-field, he shrouded himself in his faith. Whereas the partisans of the Thirty Years' War have no individual life—no idea of their own; their very breath is but the inspiration of the evil genius who urges them on. These automatons, who grow blinder every day, are not the less obstinate and bloody. No history would lead us to understand this abominable phenomenon, if there did not remain some delineation of them in the hellish pictures of that diabolical, *damned* Salvator Rosa.[4]

Behold, then, this fruit of mildness, benignity, and paternity; see how, after having by indulgence and connivance exterminated morality, seized on the family by surprise, fascinated the mother and conquered the child, and by the devil's own art raised the *man-machine*, they are found to have created a monster, whose whole idea, life, and action was *murder*, nothing more.

Wise politicians, amiable men, good fathers, who with so much mildness have skilfully arranged from afar the Thirty Years' War, seducing Aquaviva, you learned Canisius, and you good Possevino, the friend of St. François de Sales, who will not admire the flexibility of your genius? At the very time you were organising the terrible intrigue of this second and prolonged St. Bartholomew, you were mildly discussing with the good saint the difference that ought to be observed between "those who died in love, and those who died for love."

What by-path led from these mild theories to such atrocious results? How did it happen that souls enervated by gallant devotion and devout gallantry, and spoiled by the daily facilities of an obliging and accommodating casuistry, allowed themselves to be taken asleep in the meshes of political intrigue? It would be a long story. In order to set about it one must wade through their nauseous literature; but one sickens at the sight of their filthy trash.

One word, however, for it is important. Prepared as the world was, both by bad morals and bad taste, for the miserable productions with which the Jesuits inundated it, all this insipid flood would have subsided without leaving any traces behind, had they not mingled with it a part of the pure original stream, which had already delighted the human heart. The charm of St. François de Sales, his sublime spiritual union with Madame de Chantal, the holy and mild seducing influence which he had exercised over women and children, served indirectly, but very efficaciously, the purpose of this great religious intrigue.

With small morality and cheap absolution, the Jesuits could very easily corrupt consciences, but not tranquillise them. They could play, with more or less skill, upon that rich instrument Falsehood, which their institution gave them, airs of science, art, literature, and theology. But could they, with all this false fingering, produce one true note?—Not one!

But this true and gentle note was precisely that which was sounded for them by St. François. They had only to play after his method to make the false appear a little less discordant. The amiable qualities of his writings, nay, their pleasing errors, were skilfully made the most of. His taste for the minute and humble, which made him bestow a partial regard upon the lesser beings of the creation, such as little children, lambs, birds, and bees, became a precedent among the Jesuits for whatever is finical and narrow-minded, for a meanness of style and littleness of heart. The bold but innocent language of an angel, pure as light itself, who incessantly points out God in his sweetest revelation, woman suckling, and the divine mysteries of love, emboldened his imitators to make the most perilous equivocations, and was the occasion of their carrying their ambiguous terms to such a pitch, that the line of demarcation between gallantry and devotion, the lover and the spiritual father, became at length invisible.

The friend of St. François de Sales, good bishop Camus, with all his little romances, contributed much to this. There was nothing now but pious sheep-folds, devout Astreas, and ecclesiastical Amyntases. Conversion sanctifies everything in these novels; I am aware of it. The lovers at the end of the story enter a convent or seminary, but they arrive there by a long roundabout road, which enables them to dream by the way.

A taste for the romantic and insipid, the benignant and paternal style, thus gained ground rapidly. The event showed that the innocent had worked for the benefit of the cunning. A St. François and a Camus prepared the way for Father Douillet.

The essential point for the Jesuits was to reduce and to lessen, to make minds weak and false, to make the little very little, and turn the simple into idiots: a mind nourished with trifles and amused with toys must be easy to govern. Emblems, rebuses, and puns, the delight of the Jesuits, were very fit for that purpose. Among the class of silly emblems, few books can vie with the *Imago primi Soeculi Societatis Jesu.*

All this paltry nonsense succeeded admirably with women who had no sort of occupation, and whose minds had been for a long time corrupted by an unintellectual gallantry. It has been proved by experience, in every age, that to please the sex only two things are requisite; first, to amuse them, to participate in their taste for everything that is trifling, romantic, and false; secondly, to flatter them, and spoil them in their weaknesses, by making one's self weaker, more effeminate, and womanish than they.

This was the line of conduct laid down for all.—How is it that the lover gets an advantage over the husband? Generally speaking, it is less by his passion, than by his assiduity and complaisance, and by flattering woman's fancy. The director will make use of the very same means; he will flatter, and so much the more successfully, as some degree of austerity at least was expected from his character and profession. But what is to prevent another from flattering still more? We have just now seen an instance (a respectable one, it is true) of these spiritual infidelities.

In changing continually one confessor for another, merely on account of his being more gentle and indulgent than the former, we run the risk of falling very low in morality. To get the upper hand over so many accommodating directors, an entirely new standard of effeminacy and baseness is required. The new comer must entirely change the characters; and instead of being the judge, as formerly, at the bar of penitence, he must be a suppliant; justice will be obliged to plead before the sinner, and the divine man becomes the penitent!

The Jesuits, who by these means supplanted so many directors, bear witness, that in this sort of opposition they had no one to fear. They knew well enough, that no other would be found better qualified than a Jesuit for easy indulgence, disguised connivance, and subtilty to overreach the Deity. Father Cotton was so little afraid of his penitents leaving him, that, on the contrary, he used occasionally to advise them to go to the other confessors: "Go," said he, "go and try them; you will return to me!"

Only imagine this general emulation among confessors, directors, and consulting casuists, to justify everything, to find every day some adroit means of carrying indulgence still further, of declaring innocent some new case, that had hitherto been supposed guilty. The result of this manner of waging war against sin, emulously carried by so many learned men, was its gradual and universal disappearance from the common life of man; sin could no longer find a haven of refuge, and one might reasonably suppose that in a few years it would cease to exist in the world.

The great book of "Provinciales," with all the artifice of method, omits one thing, which we regret. In showing us the unanimity of the casuists, the author presents them, as it were, on the same line, and as contemporaries. It would have been more instructive to have dated them, and given to each his appointed period; and thus, according to his merits in the progressive development of casuistry, to show how they severally advanced towards perfection, outbidding, surpassing, and eclipsing one another.

In so great a rivalry, it was necessary to make every effort, and set all their wits to work. The penitent having the option, might become difficult. He wanted his absolution at a cheaper rate every day; and they who would not lower their price lost their customers. It was business that required a clever man to find out, in so great a relaxation, by what means further indulgence might be given. A fine, elastic, and indulgent science, that, instead of imposing rules, adapted itself to proportions, narrowing or widening, and taking measurement, as the case might be. Every progress of this kind, being carefully noted down served as a starting-post to go further. In countries that have once become aguish, fever produces fever; the sick inhabitant neglecting the precaution for preserving health, filth accumulates on filth, the waters form marshes, and the miasma grows stronger; a close, heavy, and noxious atmosphere oppresses the country. The people crawl or lie down. Do not speak to them of attempting any remedy; they are accustomed to the fever; they have had it on and off ever since their birth, and their forefathers had it. Why try remedies? The country has been in the same state from time immemorial; it would be almost a pity, according to these authorities, to make a change.

[1] The Apostle puts the matter thus:—
Therefore by the deeds of the law there shall no flesh be justified in His sight: for by the law is the knowledge of sin. But now the righteousness of God without the law is manifested, being witnessed by the law and the prophets; even the righteousness of God which is by faith of Jesus Christ unto all and upon all them that believe: for there is no difference: for all have sinned, and come short of the glory of God: being justified freely by His grace through the redemption that is in

Christ Jesus: whom God hath set forth to be a propitiation through faith in His blood, to declare His righteousness for the remission of sins that are past, through the forbearance of God; to declare, I say, at this time His righteousness: that He might be just, and the justifier of him which believeth in Jesus.— Rom. iii. 20-26.

[2] See in Léger, the vast system of espionage, intrigue, and secret persecution, that the first ladies of Piedmont and France had organised, under the direction of the Jesuits.

[3] Excepting the electrical moment of Gustavus-Adolphus.

[4] The term is a harsh one, and I am sorry for it. If this great artist paints war so cruelly, it is doubtless because he had more feeling than any of his contemporaries, and appreciates more keenly the horror of this terrible epoch.

CHAPTER IV.

CONVENTS.—NEIGHBOURHOOD OF CONVENTS.—
CONVENTS IN THE SEVENTEENTH CENTURY.—
CONTRAST WITH THE MIDDLE AGE.—THE DIRECTOR.—
DISPUTE ABOUT THE DIRECTION OF THE NUNS.—THE
JESUITS TRIUMPH THROUGH CALUMNY.

An ingenuous and intellectual German lady told me one day that, when she came with her husband to Paris for the first time, they had wandered about in a grand but very dull quarter of the town, where they made an infinite number of turns and windings without being able to find their way. They had entered by a public garden, and found at last another public garden that brought them out again at the quay. I saw that she meant the learned and pious neighbourhood which contains so many convents and colleges, and reaches from the Luxembourg to the "Jardin des Plantes."

"I saw," said this lady, "whole streets with gardens, surrounded with high walls, that reminded me of the deserted districts of Rome, where the *malaria* prevails, with this difference, that these were not deserted, but, as it were, mysteriously inhabited, shut up, mistrustful, and inhospitable. Other streets, exceedingly dark, were in a manner buried between two rows of lofty grey houses with no front aspect, and which showed, as it were in derision, their walled-up windows, or their rivetted lattices, turned upside down, by which one may see—nothing. We asked our way several times, and it was often pointed out to us; but somehow or other, after having gone up and down and up again, we ever found ourselves at the same point. Our *ennui* and fatigue increased. We invincibly and fatally met with the same dull streets, and the same dismal houses sullenly shut, which seemed to look at us with an evil eye. Exhausted at last, and seeing no end to the puzzle, oppressed more and more by a certain dispiriting influence that seemed to ooze from these walls, I sat down upon a stone and began to weep."

A dispiriting lassitude does indeed seize and oppress our hearts at the very sight of these disagreeable-looking houses; the most cheerful are the hospitals. Having been for the most part built or rebuilt in those times of solemn dulness, the reigns of Louis XIII. and Louis XIV., there is nothing about them to remind us of the lovely art of the *renaissance*. The latest memento of that art is the Florentine front of the Luxembourg Palace. All those houses that were built at a later period, even those which affect a certain severe luxury (the Sorbonne, for example), are occasionally great, but never grand. With their lofty pointed roofs, and stiff straight lines, they have always a dry, dull, and monotonous appearance, a *priestly* or *old-maidenish* look. In this they scarcely belie themselves, the greater part of them having been built to accommodate the numberless females belonging to the nobility and upper class of citizens, who, in order to enrich a son, condemned their unfortunate daughters to a sad, but decent death.

The monuments of the middle ages have a melancholy, but not a dispiriting look; we feel, on looking at them, the vigour and sincerity of the sentiment that inspired their builders. They are not, generally speaking, official monuments, but living works of the people, the offspring of their faith. But these, on the contrary, are nothing else than the creation of a class,—that class of newly-created nobles that swarmed into life in the seventeenth century by subserviency, the ante-chamber, and ministerial offices. They are hospitals opened for the daughters of these families. Their great number might almost deceive us as to the strength and extent of the religious re-action of that time. Look at them well, and tell me, I pray you, whether you can discern the least trace about them of the ascetic character—are they religious houses, hospitals, barracks, or colleges? There is nothing to prove what they are. They would be perfectly fit for any civil purpose. They have but one character, but it is a very decided one: serious uniformity, decent mediocrity, and *ennui.*—It is *ennui* itself, personified in an architectural form—a palpable, tangible, and visible *ennui.*

The reason of these houses being indefinitely multiplied is, that the austerity of the ancient rules having been then much modified, parents had less hesitation in making their daughters take the veil; for it was no longer burying them alive. The parlours were saloons frequented by crowds, under the pretext of being edified. Fine ladies came there to confide their secrets, filling the minds of the nuns with intrigues and vexations, and troubling them with useless regrets.

These worldly cares caused the interior of the convents to appear to them still more dismal; for there they had nothing but trifling insipid ceremonies, a sort of modified austerity, and an idle and empty routine of monotonous life.

Monastic life was quite a different thing in the middle ages; it was much more serious. There were then in the convents both more training for death, and a more active life. The system was, generally speaking, based upon two principles, which were sincerely and strictly adhered to: the destruction of the body, and the vivification of the soul. To war against the body they employed an exterminating fasting, excessive vigils, and frequent bleeding. For the development of the soul, the monks and nuns were made to read, transcribe, and sing. Up to the eleventh century they understood what they sang, as there was but little difference between Latin and the vulgar tongues of that period. The service had then a dramatic character, which sustained and constantly captivated the attention. Many things that have been reduced to simple words, were then expressed in gestures and pantomimes; what is now spoken was then *acted*. When they inflicted upon worship that serious, sober, and wearisome character that it still wears, the nuns were still allowed, as an indemnification, pious reading, legends, the lives of saints, and other books that had been translated. All these consolations were taken from them in the sixteenth century; the discovery was made, that it was dangerous to give them too great a taste for reading. In the seventeenth, even singing appeared to be an object of suspicion to many confessors; they were afraid the nuns might grow tender in singing the praises of God.[1]

But what did they give them as a substitute? What did they get in return for all those services which they no longer understood, for their reading and singing that were now denied them, and for so many other comforts, of which they were successively deprived?

Was it an inanimate object? No, it was a man; let us speak out plainly, the *director*. The director was a novelty, hardly known to the middle ages, contented with the confessor.

Yes, a man is to inherit all this vast vacant place: his conversation and teaching are to fill up the void. Prayers, reading, if it be permitted, everything, will be done according to his direction and by him. God, whom they imbibed in their books, or in their sight, even God is henceforward dispensed to them by this man—measured out to them day by day according to the standard of his heart.

Ideas come crowding here—but they must wait; we will examine them afterwards. Now they would only interrupt the thread of our historical deduction.

At the first outbreak of religious re-action, the nuns were generally governed by the friars of their order. The Bernardin nuns were directed by the Bernardin friars, the Carmelite nuns by the Carmelite friars, and the nuns of St. Elizabeth by the Picpus friars. The Capuchin nuns were not only confessed by their friars, but were fed at their expense, and by the produce of their begging.[2]

The monks did not long preserve this exclusive possession. For more than a quarter of a century, priests, monks, and friars of every order, carried on a furious war against one another on this question. This mysterious empire of shut-up and dependent women, over whom unlimited sway may be held, was, not without reason, the common aim of the ambition of all. Such houses, apparently quiet and strangers to the world, nevertheless are always *grand centres of action*. Here was an immense power for the orders that should get possession of it; and for individuals, whether priests or friars, it was (let them confess it, or not) an affair of passion.

What I say here, I say of the purest and most austere, who are often the most tender. The honourable attachment of Cardinal Bérulle for the Carmelite nuns, whom he had brought here, was know to everybody. He had lodged them near his house; he visited them every hour of the day, and even in the evening. The Jesuits said *at night*. It was to them he went when he was ill, in order to get better. When Paris was infested by a plague, he said he would not leave it, "on account of his nuns."

The Oratorians and the Jesuits, naturally enemies and adversaries, joined together at first in a common cause to remove the Carmelite friars from the direction of these nuns; but no sooner had they succeeded, than they began to dispute with each other.

The austere order of the Carmelites, which spread but little in France, obtained its importance as the *beau idéal* of penitence, a sort of religious poetry. The enthusiastic spirit of Saint Theresa still animated them. There it was that the most violent converts came to seek refuge; and there it was, also, that those whose wounds were too deep, and who, like Madame de la Vallière, sought death as their last resource, came to die.

But the two great institutions of this age, those which expressed its spirit and had an immense development, were the Visitandines and the Ursulines. The former had, in the reign of Louis XIV., about a hundred and fifty monasteries, and the latter from three to four hundred.

The Visitandines were, as is well known, the most gentle of these orders: they awaited the coming of their divine Bridegroom in a state of inaction; and their sluggish life was well calculated to make them visionaries. We know the astonishing success of Marie Alocoque, and how it was turned to account by the Jesuits.

The Ursulines, a more useful body, devoted themselves to education. In the three hundred and fifty convents which belonged to them in this century, they educated, at the smallest computation, thirty-five thousand young girls. This vast establishment for education, directed by skilful hands, might, indeed, become a political engine of enormous power.

The Ursulines and the Visitandines were governed by bishops, who appointed their confessors. St. François de Sales, so excellent a friend to the Jesuits and friars in general, had showed himself distrustful of them in the subject that was dearest to his heart, that of the Visitation:—"My opinion is (says he) that these good girls do not know what they want, if they wish to submit themselves to the superiority of the friars, who, indeed, are excellent servants of God; but it always goes hard for girls to be governed by the orders, *who are accustomed to take from them the holy liberty of the mind.*"[3]

It is but too easy to perceive how the orders of women servilely reproduced the minds of the men who directed them. Thus, the devotion of those who were governed by monks was characterised by every species of caprice, eccentricity, and violence; whilst they who were under the direction of secular priests, such as the Oratorians and the Doctrinaires, show some faint traces of reason, together with a sort of narrow-minded, common-place, and unproductive wisdom.

The nuns, who received from the bishops their ordinary confessors, chose for themselves an extraordinary one besides, who, as being extraordinary, did not fail to supplant and annul the former: the latter was, in most cases, a Jesuit. Thus the new orders of the Ursulines and Visitandines, created by priests, who had endeavoured to keep friars out of them, fell, nevertheless, under the influence of the latter: the priests sowed, but the Jesuits reaped the harvest.

Nothing did greater service to the cause of the Jesuits than their constantly repeating that their austere founder had expressly forbidden them ever to govern the convents of women. This was true, as applied to convents generally, but false as regarded nuns in particular, and their special direction. They did not, indeed, govern them *collectively*, but they directed them *individually*.

The Jesuit was not pestered with the daily detail of spiritual management, or the small fry of trifling faults. He did not fatigue; he only interfered at the right time; he was particularly useful in dispensing the nuns from telling the confessor what they wished to conceal. The latter became, by degrees, a sort of husband, whom they might disregard.

If he happened, indeed, to have any firmness in his composition, or to be able to exercise any influence, the others worked hard to get rid of him by force of calumny. We may form an opinion of the audacity of the Jesuits in this particular, since they did not fear to attack the Cardinal de Bérulle himself, notwithstanding his power.[4] One of his relatives, living with the Carmelites, having become pregnant, they boldly accused him of the crime, though he had never set his foot within the convent. Finding no one to believe them, and seeing they would gain nothing by attacking him on the score of morality, they joined in a general outcry against his books. "They contained the hidden poison of a dangerous mysticism: the cardinal was too tender, too indulgent, and too weak, both as a theologian and *a director.*" Astounding impudence! when everybody knew and saw what sort of directors they were themselves!

This, however, had, in time, the desired effect, if not against Bérulle, at least against the Oratory, who became disgusted with, and afraid of, the direction of the nuns, and at last abandoned it.

This is a remarkable example of the all-powerful effects of *Calumny*, when organised on a grand scale by a numerous body, vented by them, and continually sung in chorus. A band of thirty thousand men repeating the same thing every day throughout the Christian world! Who could resist that? This is the very essence of Jesuitical art, in which they are unrivalled. At the very creation of their order, a sentence was applied to them, similar to those well-known verses in which Virgil speaks of the Romans:—

"Excudent alii spirantia mollius æra," &c., &c.

Others shall animate brass, or give life to marble; the Romans shall excel in other arts. "Remember, Jesuit, thy art is calumny."

[1] Châteaubriand, Vie de Rancé, pp. 227-229.

[2] See Héliot; and, for Paris especially, Félibien.

[3] OEuvres, vol. xi. p. 120 (ed. 3318.)

[4] Tabaraud, Life of Bérulle, vol. i. passim.

CHAPTER V.

Morality was weakened, but not quite extinct. Though undermined by the casuists, Jesuitism, and by the intrigues of the clergy, it was saved by the laity. The age presents us this contrast. The priests, even the best of them, the Cardinal de Bérulle for instance, rush into the world, and into politics; while illustrious persons among the laity, such as Descartes and Poussin, retire to seek solitude. The philosophers turn monks, and the saints become men of business.

Each set of people will acquire what it desires in this century. One party will have power; they will succeed in obtaining the banishment of the Protestants, the proscription of the Jansenists, and the submission of the Galileans to the pope. Others will have science; Descartes and Galileo give the movements; Leibnitz and Newton furnish the harmony. That is to say, the Church will triumph in temporal affairs, and the laity will obtain the spiritual power.

From the desert where our great lay-monks then took refuge a purer breeze begins to blow. We feel that a new age now commences, modern age, the age of work, following that of disputes. No more dreams, no more school-divinity. We must now begin to work in earnest, early and before daylight. It is rather cold, but no matter; it is the refreshing coolness of the dawn, as after those beautiful nights in the North, where a young queen of twenty goes to visit Descartes, at four in the morning, to learn the application of algebra to geometry.

This serious and exalted spirit, which revived philosophy and modified literature, had necessarily some influence on theology. It found a resting point, though a very minute and still imperceptible one, in the assembly of the friends of Port-Royal; it added grandeur to their austerity, morality asserted its own claims, and religion awoke to a sense of her danger.

Everything was going on prosperously for the Jesuits; as confessors of kings, grandees, and fine ladies, they saw their morality everywhere in full bloom; when in this serene atmosphere, the lightning flashes and the thunderbolt falls. I speak of Arnaud's book, entitled "Frequent Communion" (1643), so unexpected and so overwhelming.

Not only the Jesuits and Jesuitism were struck by the blow, but, in general, all that portion of Christendom, which was enervated by an easy indulgence. Christianity appeared again austere and grave; the world again saw with awe the pale face of its crucified Saviour. He came to say again, in the name of grace, what natural reason equally asserts, "There is no real expiation without repentance." What became of all their petty arts of evasion in presence of this severe truth? What became of their worldly devotions and romantic piety, together with all the Philotheas, Erotheas, and their imitations? The contrast appeared odious.

Other writers have said, and will say, all this much better. I am not writing here the history of Jansenism. The theological question is now become obsolete. The moral question still survives, and history owes it one word, for it cannot remain indifferent between the honest and the dishonest. Whether the Jansenist did or did not exaggerate the doctrine of grace, we must still call this party, as it deserves to be, in this grand struggle, the party of virtue.

Arnaud and Pascal are so far from having gone too far against their adversaries, that one might easily show they stopped short of the mark, of their own accord, that they did not wish to make use of all their arms, and were afraid (in attacking, on certain delicate points, the Jesuitical direction) of doing harm to direction in general, and to confession.

Ferrier, the Jesuit, avows that, after the terrible blow inflicted by the *Lettres Provinciales*, the Jesuits were crushed, and that they fell into derision and contempt. A multitude of bishops condemned them, and not one stood up in their defence.

One of the means they employed to mend their case was, to say boldly that the opinions with which they were reproached were not those of the Society, but of a few individuals. They were answered that, as all their books were examined by the chief, they belonged thus to the whole body. No matter: to amuse the simple, they got a few of their order to write against their own doctrine. A Spanish Jesuit wrote against Ultramontanism. Another, the Father Gonzales, wrote a book against the casuists: he was very useful to them. When, in course of time, Rome was at last ashamed of their doctrine, and disavowed them, they put Gonzales forward, printed his book, and made him their general. Even in our own time, it is this book and this name that they oppose to us. Thus they have an answer for everything. Should you like *indulgence*, take Escobar; should you prefer *severity*, take Gonzales.

Let us now see what was the result of this general contempt into which they fell after the *Provinciales*. Public conscience having received such good warning, every one apparently will hasten to shun them. Their confession will be avoided and their colleges deserted. You think so? Then you are much mistaken.

They are too necessary to the corruption of the age. How could the king, with his two-fold adultery posted up in the face of all Europe, make his devotions without them? Fathers Ferrier, Canard, and La Chaise, will remain with him till the end, like pieces of furniture that are too convenient to be dispensed with.

But does not Rome perceive how much she is compromised by such allies? It is not incumbent on her to separate from them?

Feeble attempts were not wanting. A pope condemned the apology of the casuists that the Jesuits had risked. The energy of Rome went no further: if any remained, it was employed against the enemies of the Jesuits. The latter got the upper hand; they had succeeded, in the beginning of the century, in getting the head of the Church to impose silence on the doctrine of grace, as defended by the Dominicans; and they silenced it again, in the middle of the century, when it recommenced speaking by the mouth of the Jansenists.

The Jesuits showed their gratitude to Rome, for imposing this silence a second time, by stretching still farther the infallibility of the pope. They did not fear to build up still higher this falling Tower of Babel; they increased it by two stories: first, they asserted the infallibility of the pope *in matters of faith*. Secondly, when the danger had become imminent, they took a bold and foolish step; but it secured to them the friendship of Rome; they made the pope do in his decrepitude what he had never dared to do in his power—declare himself infallible *in matters of fact*.

And this at the very moment that Rome was obliged to confess that she was wrong about the greatest facts of nature and history. Not to speak of the New World, which she was obliged to admit, after having denied it, she condemns Galileo, and then she submits to his system, adopts and teaches it: the penance that she imposed on him for one day has, since Galileo, been inflicted upon herself for two hundred years.

Here is another fact, still graver in one sense:—

The fundamental right of popes, the title of their power, those famous Decrees which they quoted and defended, as long as criticism, unaided by the art of printing, failed to enlighten mankind;—well! the pope is obliged to confess that these very Decrees are a tissue of lies and imposture.[1]

What? when popery has disclaimed its own word, and given itself the lie on the fundamental fact, upon which its own right depends, is it then that the Jesuits claim for her infallibility in matters of fact?

The Jesuits have been the tempters and corrupters of popes as well as of kings. They caught kings by their *concupiscence*, and popes by their *pride*.

It is a laughable, but touching sight to see this poor little Jansenist party, then so great in genius and heart, resolute in making an appeal to the justice of Rome, and remaining on their knees before this mercenary judge!

The Jesuits were not so blind but that they saw that popery, foolishly propped up by them in theology, was miserably losing ground in the political world. In the beginning of the 17th century the pope was still powerful; he whipped Henry IV. in the person of the Cardinal d'Ossat. But in the middle of that century, after all the great efforts of the Thirty Years' War, the pope was not even consulted in the Treaty of Westphalia; and in that of the Pyrenees, between Catholic Spain and very-Christian France, they forgot that he existed.

The Jesuits had undertaken what was perfectly impossible; and the principal engine they employed for it—the monopoly of the rising generation—was not less impossible. Their greatest effort had been directed to this point; they had succeeded in getting into their hands the greater part of the children of the nobility and of people of fortune; they had contrived, by means of education, a machine to narrow the mind and crush the intellect. But such was the vigour of modern invention, that in spite of the most ingenious machinery to annihilate invention, the first generation produced Descartes, the second the author of Tartuffe, and the third Voltaire.

The worst of it is, by the light of this great modern flambeau which they had been unable to extinguish, they saw their own deformity. They knew what they were, and began to despise themselves. No one is so hardened in lying as to deceive himself entirely. They were obliged tacitly to confess that their *probabilism*, or doctrine of probability, was at bottom but doubt, and the absence of all principle. They could not help discovering that they, the most Christian of all societies, and the champions of the faith, were only sceptics.

Of faith?—what faith? It was not, at any rate, Christian faith: all their theology had no other tendency than to ruin the base on which Christianity is founded—grace and salvation by the blood of Jesus Christ.

Champions of a principle? No; but agents of a plot, occupied with one project, and this an impossible one—the restoration of popery.

Some few Jesuits resolved to seek a remedy in themselves for their fallen condition. They avowed frankly the urgent need that the Society had of reform. Their chief, a German, dared to attempt this reform; but it went hard with him: the great majority of the Jesuits wished to maintain the abuses, and they deprived him of all power.

These good workmen, who had been so successful in justifying the enjoyments of others, wanted to enjoy themselves in their turn. They chose for their general a man after their own heart, amiable, gentle, and kind, the epicure Oliva. Rome, recently governed by Madame Olympia, was in a season of indulgence; Oliva, retiring to his delightful villa, said, "Business to-morrow," and left the Society to govern itself after its own fashion.

Some became merchants, bankers, and cloth-makers for the profit of their establishments. Others following more closely the example of the pope, worked for their nephews, and transacted the business of their families. The idle wits frequented the public walks, coquetted, and made madrigals. Others again found amusement in chatting to the nuns, in the little secrets of women, and in sensual inquisitiveness. Their rulers, lastly, who found themselves excluded from the society of women, became too often the Thyrsis and Corydons of the Colleges; the consequence was in Germany a formidable investigation; when a great number of the proud and austere German houses were found to be criminal.

The Jesuits, who had fallen so low both in theory and practice, increased their party at the risk of the strangest auxiliaries. Whoever declared himself an enemy of the Jansenists became their friend. Hence arose the immoral inconsistency of the Society—its perfect indifference to systems. These people, who for more than half a century had been fighting for free will, formed a sudden alliance, without any intervening period of transition, with the mystics who confounded all their liberty in God. Just before they had been reproached with following the principles of pagan philosophers and jurisconsults, who attribute everything to justice and nothing to grace or love; now they receive quietism at its birth with open arms, and the preacher of love, the visionary Desmarets de St. Sorlin.

Desmarets had, it is true, done them some essential service. He had succeeded in dismembering Port-Royal, by gaining over some of the nuns. He assisted them powerfully in destroying poor Morin, another visionary more original and more innocent, who fancied himself to be the Holy Ghost. He tells us himself how, being encouraged by Father Canard (Annat) the king's confessor, he gained the confidence of this unfortunate man, made him believe he was his disciple, and drew from him written documents, by means of which he caused him to be burnt (1663).

The protection of this all-powerful confessor gained for the most extravagant books of Desmarets the approbation of the Archbishop of Paris. He declared in them that he was a prophet, and undertook to raise for the king and the pope an army of a hundred and forty-four thousand *devots*, as knights of papal infallibility, to exterminate, in concert with Spain, the Turks and the Jansenists.

These *devots*, or victims of love, were self-sacrificed people, who affected a sort of inward annihilation, and who lived henceforth only in God. Hence they could do no harm. The soul, said this prophet, having become a nonentity, cannot consent; so that whatever it may do, inasmuch as it has not consented, it has not sinned. It no longer thinks at all, either of what it has done, or of what it has not done; for it has done nothing at all. God being all in us, does all, and suffers all; the devil can no longer find the creature, either in itself or in its acts, for it acts no longer. By an entire dissolution of ourselves, the virtue of the Holy Ghost flows into us, and we become wholly God, by a miraculous *deiformity*. If there be still anything jarring in the grosser part, the purer part knows nothing of it; but both these parts, being subtilised and rarefied, change at last into God; "*God then abides with the emotions of sensuality, all of which are sanctified.*"[2]

Desmarets did not confine himself to printing this doctrine with the privilege of the king and the approbation of the archbishop. Strongly supported by the Jesuits, he ran from convent to convent preaching to the nuns. Layman as he was, he had made himself a director of female youth. He related to them his dreams of devout gallantry, and inquired about their carnal temptations. It seemed that a man so perfectly self-annihilated might write fearlessly the strangest things—the following letter for instance:—"I embrace you, my very dear love, in your nonentity, being a perfect nullity myself, each of us being all in our All, by our amiable Jesus," &c.

What progress is here made in a few years, since the "Provincial Letters!" What has become of the casuists? Those simple people who took and effaced transgressions one by one, giving themselves immense trouble. They are all scattered to the winds.

Casuistry was an art that had its masters, doctors, and cunning men. But now, what need of doctors? Every *spiritual* man, every devout person, every Jesuit in a short robe can speak as well as he in the long one the soft language of pious tenderness. The Jesuits have fallen, but *Jesuitism* has gained ground. It is no longer requisite to direct the *attention* every day, for every distinct case, by special equivocations. Love that mingles and confounds everything is the sovereign, most gentle, and powerful equivocation. Lull the *will* to sleep and there is no longer any intention, "The soul, losing its nonentity in its infinity," will be gently annihilated in the bosom of love.

[1] By two cardinals and librarians of the Vatican, Bellarmin and Baronius, one of whom was the confessor of the pope.

[2] Desmarets de St. Sorlin's Delight of the Spirit, 29th *journée*, p. 170.

CHAPTER VI.

CONTINUATION OF MORAL REACTION.—TARTUFFE, 1664-1669.—REAL TARTUFFES.—WHY TARTUFFE IS NOT YET A QUIETIST.

The devotee caught in the fact by the man of the world, the churchman excommunicated by the comedian—this is the meaning and aim of the *Tartuffe*.

Plato, in his Athenian Tartuffe (the Euthyphron), put this grand moral question, "Can there be *sanctity* without *justice*?" This question, so clear in itself but so skilfully obscured by casuists, was again put forward in open daylight. The *Theatre* re-established religious morality which had been so endangered in the *Churches*.

The author of the *Tartuffe* chose his subject, not in society in general, but in a more limited space, in the family circle, the fireside, the holy of holies of modern life. This dramatist, this impious being was, of all men in the world, the one who had most at heart the religion of the family, though he had no family himself. He was both tender and melancholy, and sometimes, in speaking of himself and his domestic griefs, he would utter this grave but characteristic sentence: "I ought to have foreseen that one thing made me unfit for family society; which is my austerity."

The *Tartuffe*, that grand and sublime picture, is very simple in its outline. Had it been more complicated it had been less popular. *Mental restriction* and the *direction of intention*, which everybody had laughed at since the "Provincial Letters," were sufficient matter for Molière. He did not venture to bring the new doctrine of mysticism on the stage, being as yet too little known or too dangerous.

Had he employed the jargon of Desmarets and the earlier quietists, and put into the mouth of Tartuffe their mystic tendernesses, the result would have been the same as that of his ridiculous sonnet in the *Misanthrope*—the pit would have wondered what it meant.

The evening before the first representation of Tartuffe, Molière read the piece to Ninon; "and to pay him back in his own coin, she related to him a similar adventure she had had with a wretch of that species, whose portrait she drew in such lively and natural colours, that if the piece had not been composed, he said he never would have undertaken it."

What, then, could be wanting to this master-piece, this drama of such profound conception and powerful execution? Nothing, certainly, but what was excluded by the state of religion at that time, and by the customs of our theatre.

Still one thing was wanting, which was impossible to be shown in so short a drama (though, in fact, it constitutes the real essence of the characters), I mean the preparatory management, the long windings by which he makes his approaches, his patience in stratagems, and his gradual fascination.

Everything is strongly told, but rather abruptly. This man, received into the house out of charity—this low rogue, this glutton who eats as much as six, this red-eared villain—how did he grow bold so suddenly and aspire so high? A declaration of love from such a man to such a lady, from an intended son-in-law to his future mother-in-law, still astonishes when we read it. On the stage, perhaps, we countenance it more easily.

Elmira, when the holy man makes this surprising avowal to her face is by no means prepared to listen to him. A real Tartuffe would have acted in a very different manner: he would have quietly sat down, humble and patient, and waited for the favourable moment. If, for instance, Elmira had experienced the indiscretions and fickleness of those worldly lovers whom Tartuffe mentions, then, indeed, when she was worn out by these trials, and become weak, weary, and dispirited, he might have accosted her; then perhaps she would have allowed him to say, in the smooth quietist jargon, many things that she cannot listen to at the moment when Molière presents her before us.

Mademoiselle Bourignon, in her curious *Life*, which well deserves another edition, relates what danger she was in through a saint of this species. I shall let her speak for herself. But first you must know that the pious damsel, who had just become an heiress, was thinking about laying out her wealth in endowing convents, and in other similar acts of piety.

"Being, one day, in the streets of Lille, I met a man whom I did not know, who said to me as he passed, 'You will not do what you wish; you will do what you do not wish.' Two days after, the same man came to my house and said, 'What did you think of me?' 'That you were either a fool or a prophet,' replied I. 'Neither,' said he; 'I am a poor fellow from a village near Douai, and my name is Jean de St. Saulieu; I have no other thought but that of charity. I lived first of all with a hermit, but now I have my curé, Mr. Roussel, for a director. I teach poor children to read. The sweetest— the most charitable act you could do would be to collect all the little female orphans; they have become so numerous since the wars! The convents are rich enough.' He spoke for three hours together with much unction.

"I inquired about him of the curé, his director, who assured me that he was a person of a truly apostolical zeal. (We should observe that the curé had tried at first to catch this rich heiress for his own nephew; the nephew not succeeding, he employed one of his own creatures.) Saint Saulieu frequently repeated his visits, speaking divinely of spiritual things. I could not understand how a man without any preparatory study could speak in so sublime a manner of the divine mysteries. I believed him to be really inspired by the Holy Ghost. He said himself that he was dead to nature. He had been a soldier, and had returned from the wars as chaste as a child. By dint of abstinence he had lost the taste of food, and could no longer distinguish wine from beer! He passed the greater part of his time on his knees in the churches. He was seen to walk in the street with a modest air and downcast eyes, never looking at anything, as if he had been alone in the world. He visited the poor and sick, giving away all he possessed. In winter time, if he saw a poor man without a garment, he would draw him aside, take off his own coat, and give it him. My heart overflowed with joy to see that there were still such men in the world. I thanked God, and thought I had found the counterpart of myself. Priests and other pious persons put the same confidence in him, went to consult him, and receive his good advice.

"It was quite foreign to my feelings to quit my peaceful retreat, and establish the asylum for children that Saint Saulieu had recommended to me. But he brought me a tradesman who had begun the same thing, and who offered me a house where he had already located a few poor girls. I took possession in November, 1653. I cleaned these children. They were shockingly dirty, but after a great deal of trouble, I cleaned them myself, having nobody with me who liked the occupation. But at last I made a rule, and followed it myself, putting every thing in common, and making every one eat at the same table. I kept myself as retired as I could; but I was obliged to speak to all sorts of persons. Friars came, as well as devotees whose conversations did not much please me... I was frequently sick to death.

"The house in which Saint Saulieu taught having been destroyed, and himself sent away, he went to live with the tradesman of whom I have already spoken. They solicited me to make an asylum, like mine, for boys. In order to raise a necessary fund, Saint Saulieu was to take an office in the town on lease, that brought in two thousand francs a-year, and the revenue was to be applied to this foundation, myself being security for him. He received the produce of one year, and then said it was necessary, before anything was done, to receive for another year, to furnish the house. This made four thousand franks; and when he had got six thousand, he kept the whole, saying it was the fruit of his labour, and that he had well earned it.

"I had not waited for this to make me distrustful of the man; I had had some strange inward misgivings on his account. One day methought I saw a black wolf sporting with a white lamb. Another day it was the heart of Saint Saulieu, and a little Moorish child with a crown and sceptre of gold sitting upon it, as if the devil had been the king of his heart. I did not conceal these visions from him; but he grew angry, and said I ought to confess myself, for thinking so badly of my neighbour; that he could not be a black wolf; for, on the contrary, the more he approached me, the more pure and chaste he became.

"One day, however, he told me that we ought to be married, only for spiritual love; and that such a union would enable us to do still more good. To this I answered, that marriage was not requisite for such a union. He made me, however, little demonstrations of friendship, to which, at first, I paid no attention. At last, he suddenly threw off the mask, told me he loved me desperately; that for many years he had studied spiritual books, the better to win me; and that now having so much access to me, I must be his wife, either by love or force and he approached to caress me. I was very angry, and commanded him to go. Then he burst into tears, fell on his knees, and said, 'The devil tempted me.' I was simple enough to believe and to pardon him.

"This was not the end of the affair: he was always recommencing his attack, following me everywhere, and entering my house in spite of my girls. He went so far as to hold a knife to my throat to force me to yield... At the same time he said everywhere that he had gained his suit, and that I was his promised wife. I complained in vain to his confessor; I then appealed to justice, who allowed me two men to guard my house, and began an enquiry. Saint Saulieu soon absconded from Lille, and went to Ghent, where he found one of my girls, who was a great devotee and passed for a mirror of perfection: he lived with her, and she became *enceinte*. The way he arranged the Lille affair was this: he had a brother among the Jesuits, and they employed their friends so well, that he got off by paying the costs of justice, retracting his calumny, and acknowledging that I was an honest women."[1]

This took place between 1653 and 1658, consequently only a few years before the representation of Molière's *Tartuffe*, who wrote the three first acts in 1664. Everything leads us to believe that such adventures were not rare at that period. Tartuffe, Orgon, and all the other personages of this truly historical piece, are not abstract beings, pure creations of art, like the heroes of Corneille or Racine; they are real men, caught in the act, and taken from nature.

What strikes us in Mademoiselle de Bourignon's Flemish Tartuffe is his patience to study and learn mysticism in order to speak its language; and, again, his perseverance in associating himself for whole years with the thoughts of the pious maiden.

If Molière had not been confined in so narrow a frame, if his *Tartuffe* had had the time to prepare better his advances, if he had been able (the thing was then, no doubt, too dangerous) to take the cloak of Desmarets and Quietism in its birth, he might have advanced still further in his designs without being discovered. Then he would not in the very beginning have made to the person he wants to seduce the very illogical confession, that he is a cheat. He would not have ventured the expression, "If it be only heaven" (Act iv. scene 5). Instead of unmasking abruptly this ugly corruption, he would have varnished it over, and unveiled it by degrees. From one ambiguous phrase to another, and by a cunning transition, he would have contrived to make corruption take the appearance of perfection. Who knows? He might perhaps at last have succeeded, like many others, in finding it unnecessary to be a hypocrite any longer, and have finished by imposing on himself, cheating and seducing himself into the belief that he was a saint. It is then he would have been Tartuffe in the superlative degree, being so not only for the world, but for himself, having perfectly confounded within himself every ray of good, and reposing in evil with a tranquillity secured by his ignorance, counterfeit at first, but afterwards become natural.

[1] The two accounts given by Mademoiselle de Bourignon are abridged and united. See at the end of Vol. I. of her OEuvres (Amsterdam, 1686), pp. 68-80, and pp. 188-197.

CHAPTER VII.

APPARITION OF MOLINOS, 1675.—HIS SUCCESS AT HOME.—
FRENCH QUIETISTS.—MADAME GUYON.—HER
DIRECTOR.—THE TORRENTS.—MYSTIC DEATH.—DO WE
RETURN FROM IT?

The Spiritual Guide of Molinos appeared at Rome in 1675. The way
having been prepared for twenty years by different publications of the same
tendency, highly approved of by the inquisitors of Rome and Spain, this
book had a success unparalleled in the age; in twelve years it was translated
and reprinted twenty times.

We must not be surprised that this guide to annihilation, this method
to die, was received so greedily. There was then throughout Europe a
general feeling of wearisomeness. That century, still far from its close,
already panted for repose. This appears to be the case by its own doctrines.
Cartesianism, which gave it an impulse, became inactive and contemplative
in Mallebranche (1674). Spinosa, as early as 1670, had declared the
immobility of God, man, and the world, in the unity of substance. And in
1676, Hobbes gave his theory of political fatalism.

Spinosa, Hobbes, and Molinos—death, everywhere, in metaphysics,
politics, and morality! What a dismal chorus! They are of one mind without
knowing each other or forming any compact; they seem, however, to shout
to each other from one extremity of Europe to the other!

Poor human liberty has nothing left but the choice of its suicide;
either to be hurled by logic in the North into the bottomless pit of Spinosa,
or to be lulled in the South by the sweet voice of Molinos, into a death-like
and eternal slumber.

The age is, however, as yet in all its brilliancy and triumph. Some time
must pass away before these discouraging and deadly thoughts pass from
theory to practice, and politics become infected with this moral languor.

It is a delicate and interesting moment in every existence, that middle
term between the period of increasing vigour and that of old age, when,
retaining its brilliancy, it loses its strength, and decay imperceptibly begins.
In the month of August the trees have all their leaves, but soon they change
colour, many a one grows pale, and in their splendid summer robe you have
a presentiment of their autumnal decline.

For some time an impure and feverish wind had blown from the South, both from Italy and Spain: Italy was already too lifeless, too deeply entombed to be able to produce even a doctrine of death. It was a Spaniard, established at Rome and imbued with Italian languor, who invented this theory and drew it forth into practice. Still it was necessary for his disciples to oblige him to write and publish. Molinos had, for twenty years, been satisfied with sowing his doctrine noiselessly in Rome, and propagating it gently from palace to palace. The theology of Quietism was wonderfully adapted to the city of catacombs, the silent city, where, from that time, scarcely anything was heard but the faint rustling of worms crawling in the sepulchre.

When the Spaniard arrived in Rome, it had hardly recovered from the effeminate pontificate of Madame Olympia. The *crucified Jesus* reposed in the delicate hands of her general Oliva, among sumptuous *vines*, exotic flowers, lilies, and roses. These torpid Romans, this idle nobility, and these lazy fair ones, who pass their time on couches, with half-closed eyes, are the persons to whom Molinos comes at a late hour to speak—ought I to say *speak*? His low whispering voice, sinking into their lethargy, is confounded with their inward dream.

Quietism had quite a different character in France. In a living country, the theory of death showed some symptoms of life. An infinite measure of activity was employed to prove that action was no longer necessary. This injured their doctrine, for noise and light were hurtful to it. This delicate plant loved darkness and sought to grow in the shade. Not to speak of the chimerical Desmarets, who could but render an opinion ridiculous, Malaval seemed to have an idea that this new doctrine outstepped Christianity. Concerning the words of Jesus, "*I am the way*," he uses an expression surprising for this century: "Since He is the way, let us pass by Him; *but he who is always passing never arrives.*"

Our French Quietists by their lucid analysis, their rich and fertile developments, made known, for the first time, what had scarcely been dreamed of in the obscure form which Quietism had prudently preserved in other countries. Many things, that seemed in the bud hardly developed, appeared in Madame Guyon in full bloom, as clear as daylight, with the sun in the meridian. The singular purity of this woman rendered her intrepid in advancing the most dangerous ideas. She was as pure in her imagination as she was disinterested in her motives. She had no need to figure to herself the object of her pious love, under a material form. This is what gives her mysticism a sublime superiority over the coarse and sensual devotion of the *Sacré-Coeur*, established by the *Visitandine*, Marie Alacoque, about the same period. Madame Guyon was far too intellectual to give a form to her God; she truly loved a spirit; hence sprang her confidence and unlimited courage.

She attempts bravely, but without suspecting herself to be brave, the most perilous paths, now ascending, now descending into regions that others had most avoided; she presses boldly forward past the point where every one had stopped through fear, like the luminary which brightens everything and remains unsullied itself. These courageous efforts, though innocent in so pure a woman, had nevertheless a dangerous effect upon the weak-minded. Her confessor, Father Lacombe, was wrecked in this dangerous gulf, where he was swallowed up and drowned. The person and the doctrine had equally deranged his faculties. All we know of his intercourse with her betrays a strange weakness, which she, in her sublime aspirations, seems hardly to have condescended to notice. The very first time he saw her, then young, and tending her aged husband, he was so affected by the sight that he fainted. Afterwards, having become her humble disciple, under the name of her director, he followed her everywhere in her adventurous life, both in France and Savoy. He never left her side, "and could not dine without her." He had succeeded in getting her portrait taken. Being arrested at the same time as herself, in 1687, he was for ten years a prisoner in the fortresses of the Pyrenees. In 1698, they took advantage of the weakness of his mind to make him write to Madame Guyon a compromising letter: "The poor man," said she, laughing, "is become mad." He certainly was so, and, a few days after, he died at Charenton.

This madness little surprises me, when I read Madame Guyon's *Torrents*, that fantastic, charming, but fearful book. It must not be passed over in silence.

When she composed the book, she was at Annecy, in the convent of the *newly converted*. She had bestowed her wealth upon her family, and the small income she reserved for herself was also given away by her to this religious establishment, where she was very ill used. This delicate woman, who had passed her life in luxury, was forced to work with her hands beyond her strength; her employment was washing and sweeping. Father Lacombe, then in Rome, had recommended her to write whatever came into her mind. "It is to obey you," says she, "that I am beginning to write what I do not know myself." She takes a ream of paper, and writes down the title of her subject:—*Torrents*.

As the torrents of the Alps, the rivers, rivulets, and mountain streams, which tumble from their heights, rush with all their force towards the sea, even so our souls, by the effect of their spiritual inclination, hasten to return towards God to be blended with Him. This comparison of living waters is not a simple text that serves her for a starting-point; she follows it up almost throughout the volume with renewed graces. One would suppose that this pleasing light style would tire us at last; but it does not: we feel that it is not mere words and language, but that it springs and flows like life-blood from the heart. She is evidently an uninformed woman, who has read only the Imitation, the Philothea of Saint François, some few stories, and Don Quixote; knows nothing at all, and has not seen much. Even these *Torrents*, which she describes, are not seen by her in the Alps, where she then is; she sees them within herself; she sees nature in the mirror of her heart.

In reading this book we seem absolutely as if we were on the brink of a cascade, pensively listening to the murmuring of the waters. They fall for ever and ever gently and charmingly, varying their uniformity by a thousand changes of sound and colour. Thence you see the approach of waters of every sort (images of human souls), rivers that flow only to reach other broad majestic streams, all loaded with boats, goods, and passengers, and that are admired and blessed for the services they render. These streams are the souls of the saints and great doctors. There are also more rapid and eager waters which are good for nothing, on which no one dares to float, that rush forward, in headlong impatience, to reach the ocean. Such waters have terrible falls, and occasionally grow impure. Sometimes they disappear.—Alas! poor torrent, what has become of thee? It is not lost; it returns to the surface, but only to be lost again; it is yet far from its goal; it will have first to be dashed against rocks, scattered abroad, and, as it were, annihilated!

When the writer has brought her torrent to this supreme fall, she is at fault about the simile of the living waters; she then leaves it, and the torrent becomes a soul again. No image taken from nature could express what this soul is about to suffer. Here begins a strange drama, where it seems no one before had dared to venture—that of mystic death. We certainly find in earlier books a word here and there upon this dark subject; but no one yet had reached the same depth in the tomb, that deep pit where the soul is about to be buried. Madame Guyon indulges in a sort of pleasure, or perseverance, I had almost said eagerness, to grope still lower, to find, beyond all funereal ideas, a more definite death, a death more decidedly dead.

There are many things in it, that we should never have expected from a woman's hand: passion in its transports forgets reserve. This soul, that is destined to perish, must first be divested, by her divine lover, of her trappings, the gifts that had ornamented her: he snatches off her garments, that is to say, the virtues in which she had been enveloped.—O shame! She sees herself naked, and knows not where to hide! This is not yet enough; her beauty is taken away. O horror! She sees she is ugly. Frightened and wandering, she runs and becomes loathsome. The faster she runs towards God, "the more she is soiled by the dirty paths she must travel in." Poor, naked, ugly, and deformed, she loses a taste for everything, understanding, memory, and will; lastly, she loses together with her will a something or other "that is her favourite," and would be a substitute for all—the idea that she is a child of God. This is properly the death at which she must arrive at last. Let nobody, neither the director nor any other, attempt to relieve her. She must die, and be put in the ground; be trodden under foot and walked upon, become foul and rotten, and suffer the stench of corruption, until rottenness becoming dust and ashes, hardly anything may remain to testify that the soul ever existed.

What was the soul must, if it still thinks, apparently think that all it can now do is, to remain motionless in the bosom of the earth. Now, however, it begins to feel something surprising! Has the sun darted a ray through a crack in the tomb? perhaps only for one moment? No: the effect is durable, the dead soul revives, recovers some strength, a sort of life. But this is no longer her own life, it is *life in God*. She has no longer anything of her own, neither will nor desire. What has she to do to possess what she loves? Nothing, nothing, eternally nothing. But can she have any defects in this state? Doubtless she has; she knows them, but does nothing to get rid of them: to be able to do so, she would have to become as before, "thoughtful about herself." These are little mists which she must allow to disappear gradually. The soul has now God for soul; He is now become her principle of life, *He is one and identical* with her.

"In this state nothing extraordinary happens, no visions, revelations, ecstasies, nor transports. All such things do not belong to this system, which is simple, pure, and naked, seeing nothing but in God, *as God sees Himself*, and by His eyes."

Thus, after many immoral and dangerous things, the book ends in a singular purity, which few mystics have even approached. A gentle new birth, without either visions or ecstasies, and a sight divinely pure and serene, is the lot of that soul, which has passed through all the various shadows of death.

If we listen to Madame Guyon, our life, after having been crushed, soiled, and destroyed, will revive in God. He who has passed through all the horror of the sepulchre, whose living body has become a corpse, which has held communion with worms, and from rottenness has become ashes and clay—even he will resume his life, and again bloom in the sun.

What can be less credible, or less conformable to nature? She deceives herself and us by equivocal terms. The life she promises us after this death is not our own; our personality extinguished, effaced, and annihilated, will be succeeded by another, infinite and perfect, I allow; but still not ours.

I had not yet read the *Torrents* when all this was, for the first time, represented to my mind. I was ascending St. Gothard, and had advanced to meet the violent Reuss that rushes madly down the mountain in its headlong course. My imagination conjured up, in spite of myself, the terrible strugglings with which it labours to force its way through rocks that would hem it in and bar its progress. I was frightened at its falls and the efforts it seemed to make, like a poor soul on the rack, to fly from itself, and hide where it might be seen no more. It writhes at the Devil's Bridge, and, in the midst of its agony, hurled from an immense height to the bottom of the abyss, it ceases for a moment to be a river: it becomes a tempest between heaven and earth, an icy vapour, a horrible frosty blast, that fills the dark valley with an infernal mist. Mount higher and higher still. You traverse a cavern, and pass a hollow rock. Lo! the uproar ceases; this grand battle of the elements is over. Peace and silence reign. And life?—is it renewed? Do you find a new-birth after this death-struggle? The meadow is blighted, the flowers are gone, and the very grass is scarce and poor. Nothing in nature stirs, not a bird in the air, not an insect on the earth. You see the sun again, it is true, but void of rays and heat.

CHAPTER VIII.

FENELON AS DIRECTOR.—HIS QUIETISM.—MAXIMS OF SAINTS, 1697.—FENELON AND MADAME DE LA MAISONPORT.

Madame Guyon was not apparently the extravagant and chimerical person that her enemies pretend, since, on her arrival at Paris from Savoy, she managed to captivate and secure, at her first onset, the man, of all others, the most capable of giving a relish to her doctrines—a man of genius, who, moreover, had an infinite fund of sagacity and address, and who, independently of all these merits, possessed what had dispensed, if necessary, with every other qualification, being, at that time, the director the most in vogue.

This new Chantal required a St. François de Sales; she found one in Fenelon, who was less serene and innocent, it is true, and less refulgent with boyhood and seraphic grace, but eminently noble and shrewd, subtle, eloquent, close, very devout, and very intriguing.

She laid her hands upon him, seized and carried him by an easy assault. This great genius, whose mind was stored with every variety and every contradiction, would probably have continued to waver, had it not been for this powerful impulse that forced him all on one side. Till then he had wandered between different opinions, and opposite parties and communities, so that every one claimed him as his own, and thought to possess him. Though assiduous in courting Bossuet, whose disciple he said he was, never leaving his side in his retirement at Meaux, he was not less friendly to the Jesuits, and, between the two, he still held fast to Saint-Sulpice. In his theology, at one time inclining towards Grace, at another towards Free-will, imbued with the oldest mystics, and full of the presentiments of the eighteenth century, he seems to have had, beneath his faith, some obscure corners of scepticism which he was unwilling to fathom. All these divers elements, without being able to combine, were harmonised in his outward actions, under the graceful influence of the most elegant genius that was ever met with. Being both a Grecian and a Christian, he reminds us at the same time of the fathers, philosophers, and romancers of the Alexandrian period; and sometimes our sophist turns prophet, and, in his sermon, soars on the wings of Isaiah.

Everything inclines us to believe, for all that, that the astonishing writer was the least part of Fenelon—he was superlatively the *Director*. Who can say by what enchantment he bewitched souls, and filled them with transport? We perceive traces of it in the infinite charms of his correspondence, disfigured and adulterated as it is;[1] no other has been more cruelly pruned, purged, and designedly obscured. Yet in these fragments and scattered remains, seduction is still omnipotent: besides a nobleness of manner, and an animated and refined turn of thought, in which the man of power is very perceptible under the robe of the apostle, there is also what is particularly his own, a feminine delicacy that by no means excludes strength, and even in his subtilty an indescribable tenderness that touches the heart. When a youth, and before he was tutor to the Duke of Burgundy, he had, for a long time, directed the *newly converted*. There he had the opportunity of well studying woman's character, and of acquiring that perfect knowledge of the female heart, in which he was unrivalled.

The impassioned interest they took in his fortune, the tears of his little flock, the Duchesses of Chevreuse, Beauvilliers, and others, when he missed the archbishopric of Paris, their constant fidelity to this well-beloved guide during his exile at Cambrai, which ended only with his death—all this fills up the void of the lost letters, and conveys a strange idea of this all-powerful magician, whose invincible magic defied every attack.

To introduce spirituality so refined and so exalted, and such a pretension to supreme perfection into that world of outward propriety and ceremonial at Versailles, and this, at the end of a reign in which everything seemed rigidly frozen—was, indeed, a rash undertaking. There was no question here of abandoning one's self, like Madame Guyon in her retreat among the Alps, to the torrents of divine love. It was necessary to have the appearance of common sense, and the forms of reason even in the madness of love; it was expedient, as the ancient comic writer says "*to run mad with rule and measure.*" This is what Fenelon attempted to do in the *Maxims of Saints*. The condemnation of Molinos, and the imprisonment of Madame Guyon at Vincennes, were a sufficient lesson: he declared himself, but with prudence, and though perfectly decided, maintained an outward show of weak indecision.

Nevertheless, with all his skill, cunning, and prevarication, if he differs from the absolute Quietists whom he affects to condemn, it is less in any fundamental part of doctrine, than the degree in which he admits that doctrine. He thinks he goes far enough in saying, that the state of quiet in which the soul loses its activity is not a *perpetually*, but an *habitually* passive state. But in acknowledging inaction to be both superior to action and a state of perfection, does he not make us wish that the inaction might be perpetual?

The soul *habitually* passive, according to him, is concentrated above, leaving beneath her the inferior part, whose acts are those of an entirely *blind* and involuntary commotion. *These acts being always supposed to be voluntary*, he avows that the superior part still remains responsible for them. Will they then be governed by it? By no means; it is absorbed in its sublime quietude. What, then, is to interfere in its place? What is to keep order in this lower sphere, where the soul no longer descends? He tells us plainly— *it is the director.*

His modification of Molinos in theory is less important than it seems to be. The speculative part, with which Bossuet is so much occupied, is not the most essential in a point where practice is so directly interested. What is really serious is, that Fenelon, as well as Molinos, after having traced out a great plan of regulations, has not enough of these rules; he has to call in, at every moment, the assistance of the director. He establishes a system; but this system cannot work alone; it wants the hand of man. This inert theory continually requires the supplement of an especial consultation, and an empirical expedient. The director is a sort of supplementary soul for the soul, who, whilst this last is sleeping in its sublime sphere, is leading and regulating every thing for it in this miserable world below, which is, after all, that of reality.

Man, eternally man! this is what you find at the bottom of their doctrines in sifting and compressing them. This is the *ultima ratio* of their systems. Such is their theory, and such their life also.

I leave these two illustrious adversaries, Fenelon and Bossuet, to dispute about ideas. I prefer to observe their practice. There, I see that the doctrine has but a little, and man a very great part. Whether Quietists or Anti-quietists, they do not differ much in their method of enveloping the soul, and lulling the will to sleep.

During this contention of theories, or rather before it began, there was a personal one, very curious to witness. The stake in this game, if I may use the expression, the spiritual prize that both sides disputed, was a woman, a charming soul, full of transport and youth, of an imprudent vivacity, and ingenuous loyalty. She was a niece of Madame Guyon, a young lady whom they called Madame de la Maisonfort, for she was a canoness. This noble, but poor young lady, ill-treated by her father and stepmother, had fallen into the cold political hands of Madame de Maintenon. Either for the vanity of founding, or in order to amuse an old king rather difficult to entertain, she was then establishing Saint-Cyr, for the daughters of noble families. She knew the king was ever *sensible* to women, and consequently let him see only old ones or children. The boarders of Saint-Cyr, who in the innocency of their sports gladdened the eyes of the old man, brought to his mind a former age, and offered him a mild and innocent opportunity for paternal gallantry.

Madame de Maintenon, who, as is well known, owed her singular fortune to a certain decent harmony of middling qualities, looked out for an eminently middling person, if one may use the expression, to superintend this establishment. She could not do better than to seek him among the Sulpicians and Lazarists. Godet, the Sulpician, whom she took as director both of Saint-Cyr and herself; was a man of merit, though a downright pedant; at least Saint Simon, his admirer, gives us this sort of definition of him. Madame de Maintenon saw in him the blunt matter-of-fact priest, who might insure her against every sort of eccentricity. With such a man as that, one would have nothing to fear: having to choose between the two men of genius who influenced Saint-Cyr, Racine the Jansenist, and Fenelon the Quietist, she preferred Godet.

Those who are ignorant of its history would have only to look at the mansion of Saint-Cyr, to discern in it at once the real abode of *ennui*. The soul of the foundress, the domineering spirit of the governess, is everywhere perceptible. The very look of the place makes one yawn. It would be something, if this building had but a sorrowful character; even sadness may entertain the soul. No, it is not sad, yet it is not the more cheerful on that account; there is nothing to be said against it, the character and the style being equally null; there is nothing one can even blame. Of what age is the chapel? Neither Gothic nor the *renaissance*, nor is it even the Jesuit style. Perhaps, then, there is something of the Jansenist austerity? It is by no means austere. What is it then? Nothing. But this nothing causes an overwhelming *ennui*, such as one would never find elsewhere.

After this first short half-devout and half-worldly period, that of the representations of Athalie and Esther, which the young ladies had played too well, the school being reformed, became a sort of convent. Instead of Racine, it was the Abbé Pellegrin and Madame de Maintenon who wrote pieces for Saint-Cyr; and the governesses were required to be nuns. This was a great change; it displeased Louis XIV. himself, and ran the risk of compromising the new establishment. Madame de Maintenon seems to have been aware of this, and she looked out for a *foundation-stone to her edifice*, a living one—alas! a woman full of grace and life!—It was poor Maisonfort, whom they decided to veil, immure, and seal up for ever in the foundations of Saint-Cyr.

But she whose will was law in everything, was unable to do this. Lively and independent as was La Maisonfort, all the kings and queens in the world would have been unsuccessful. The heart alone, skilfully touched, was able to induce her to take the desired step. Madame de Maintenon, who desired it extremely, made such vigorous efforts, that they surprise us when we read her letters. That very reserved person throws her character aside in this business: she becomes confiding, in order to be confided in, and does not fear to avow to the young girl, whom she wishes to make disgusted with this life, that she herself, in the highest station in the world, "is dying of sadness and *ennui.*"

What proved to be much more efficacious, was their employing against her a new director, the seducing, charming, irresistible Abbé de Fenelon. He was then on very good terms with Madame de Maintenon; dining every Sunday with her in the apartments of the Duchesses de Beauvilliers and de Chevreuse, where, all alone, without servants, they served themselves, that they might not be overheard. The inclination La Maisonfort felt for this singular man was great, and authority ordered her to follow this inclination: "See the Abbé de Fenelon," Madame de Maintenon would write to her, "and accustom yourself to live with him."

Kind order! she followed it but too well:—sweet custom!—With such a man, who animated everything by his personal charm, who simplified and facilitated the most arduous things, she did not walk, but fly, between heaven and earth, into the tepid regions of divine love. So much seduction, sanctity, and liberty at once—it was too much for her poor heart!

St. Simon tells us by what method of espionage and treason Godet proved the presence of Quietism in Saint-Cyr. There was no need of so much cunning. La Maisonfort was so pure as to be imprudent. In the happiness of this new spirituality, into which she entered with her whole soul, she said much more than was required of her.

Fenelon, suspected as he had then become, was still left with her, till she had made the important step. They waited till, under his influence, and in spite of her own protestations and tears, she had taken the veil, and heard the fatal grate shut behind her.

Two meetings were held at Saint-Cyr, to decide on the destiny of the victim. Godet, supported by the Lazarists, Thiberge, and Brisacier, decided she should be a nun, and Fenelon, who was a member of this fine council, made no opposition. She herself has informed us, that, during the deliberation, "she retired before the holy sacrament in a strange agony; that she thought she should have died of grief, and that she passed the whole of the night in a flood of tears."

The deliberation was merely a matter of form; Madame de Maintenon was resolved; and obey they must. Nobody at that time was more at her command than Fenelon. It was then the decisive crisis of Quietism. The question was no less than to know whether its doctor, writer, and prophet, unpalatable as he was to the king, who, however, did not yet thoroughly know him, would be able to acquire, before his doctrine burst forth, that position of a great prelate in the church, to which all his supporters were hurrying him. Hence sprung his unlimited devotedness to Madame de Maintenon, and the sacrifice of poor Maisonfort to her omnipotent will. Fenelon, who knew perfectly well how little she was inclined to this vocation, sacrificed her, certainly not to his personal interests, but for the advancement of his doctrines and the aggrandizement of his own party.

As soon as she had taken the veil, and was immured for ever, he became more and more distant; for she was frankness itself, and by her imprudence did harm to his doctrine, which was already sharply attacked. He did not need so compromising an alliance, but what he wanted was political support. In his last extremity he addressed himself to the Jesuits, and took one of them for his confessor; for they had taken the precaution to have some on both sides.

To fall back from Fenelon to Godet, and undergo his blunt and harsh direction, was more than the new nun could support. One day, when he came to her with the little decrees and petty regulations which he had composed with Madame de Maintenon, La Maisonfort could contain herself no longer, but spoke out, before him and the all-powerful foundress, all the contempt she felt for them. A short time after, a letter with the king's seal expelled her unfeelingly from Saint-Cyr.

She had defended herself too successfully against such persons as Godet, Brisacier, and others of the hostile party. Though abandoned by Fenelon, she endeavoured to remain faithful to his doctrines, and was determined to keep his books. They were obliged to invoke the most powerful man of the time, Bossuet, in order to bring the rebel to reason. But she would not receive even his advice, till after she had asked Fenelon whether she might do so. He replies to this last mark of confidence, I regret to say, by a dull, disagreeable letter, in which are shown but too plainly his jealousy, and the regret he feels in seeing one, whom he had abandoned, pass under the control of another.

[1] A bishop, at that time an inspector of the University, boasted before me (and several other persons, who will be witnesses if necessary) that he had burned some of Fenelon's letters.

CHAPTER IX.

BOSSUET AS DIRECTOR.—BOSSUET AND SISTER CORNUAU.— HIS LOYALTY AND IMPRUDENCE.—HE IS PRACTICALLY A QUIETEST.—DEVOUT DIRECTION INCLINES TO QUIETISM.—A MORAL PARALYSIS.

Nothing throws more light upon the real character of *direction* than the correspondence of the worthiest and most loyal of directors—I mean Bossuet. Experience is decisive; if here, too, the results are bad, we must blame the method and the system, but by no means the man.

The greatness of his genius, and the nobleness of his character would naturally remove Bossuet far from the petty passions of the vulgar herd of directors, their meanness, jealousy, and vexatious tyranny. We may believe what one of his own penitents says of him:—"Without disapproving," says she, "of the directors who interfere even in the slightest thoughts and affections, *he did not relish this practice* towards those souls which loved God and had made some progress in spiritual life."

His correspondence is praiseworthy, noble, and serious. You will not find in it the too loving tenderness of Saint François de Sales, and still less the refinement and impassioned subtilties of Fenelon. Bossuet's letters, though less austere, resemble those of Saint-Cyran by their seriousness. They often contain a grandeur of style little suited to the humble and ordinary person to whom they are generally addressed, but very advantageous in keeping her at a distance, and preventing too close an intimacy even in the most unreserved private conversation.

If this correspondence has reached us in a more complete form than that of Fenelon, we are indebted for it (at least for the most curious part of it) to the veneration which one of Bossuet's penitents, the good Widow Cornuau, entertained for his memory. That worthy person, in transmitting these letters to us, has religiously left in them a number of details, humiliating enough for herself. She has forgotten her own vanity, and thought only of the glory of her spiritual father. In this, she has been very happily guided by her attachment for him; perhaps, indeed, she has done more for him than any panegyrist. These noble letters written in such profound secrecy, and never intended to see daylight, are worthy of being exhibited to the public.

This good widow tells us, that when she had the happiness of going to see him in his retirement at Meaux, he received her occasionally "in a small, very cold, and smoky room." This is, according to all appearances, the small summer-house, which is shown even in our time, at the end of the garden, on the old rampart of the city, which forms the terrace of the episcopal palace. The cabinet is on the ground-floor, and above it, in a small loft, slept the valet, who awoke Bossuet early every morning. A dark narrow alley of yews and holly leads to this dull apartment: these are old dwarf stunted trees, which have entwined their knotty branches and their dark prickly leaves. Dreams of the past dwell for ever here; here you may still find all the difficulties of those grand polemical questions, now so remote from us, the disputes of Jurien and Claude, with the stately history of the Variations, and the deadly battle of Quietism, envenomed by betrayed friendship. The tower of the cathedral, with its mild majestic mien, hovers above the French-fashioned, grave-looking garden; but it is neither seen from the dark little alley, nor from the dull cabinet; a place confined, cold, and of a disagreeable aspect, which in spite of noble reminiscences, disheartens us by its vulgarity, and reminds us that this fine genius, the best priest of his age, was still a *Priest*.

There was scarcely any other point by which this domineering spirit could be touched, than docility and obedience. The good Cornuau exercised these qualities in a degree he could hardly have expected. She gives much, and we see that she hides still more, for fear of displeasing him. She set all her wits to work, to follow, as far as her natural mediocrity permitted her, the tastes and ideas of this great man. He had a genius for government; and she had it also in miniature. She took upon herself the business of the community with which she lived, and at the same time transacted that of her own family. She waited in this manner fifteen years before she was allowed to become a nun. She at last obtained this favour, and had herself called the Sister of Saint-*Benigné*, thus assuming, rather boldly perhaps, Bossuet's own name. These real cares, in which the prudent director kept her a long time, had an excellent effect upon her, in diverting and pruning her imagination. She was of an impassioned, honest, but rather ordinary disposition; and, unfortunately for her, she had enough good sense to confess to herself what she was. She knows, and she tells herself, that she is only a commoner of the lower order; that she has neither birth, wit, grace, nor connection; that she has not even seen Versailles! What chance would she have of gaining his favour in a struggle against the other spiritual daughters, those fine ladies, ever brilliant even in their penitence and voluntary abasement?

It seems that she had hoped at first to have her revenge in some other way, and to rise above these worldly ladies by the path of mysticism. She took it into her head one day to have visions: she wrote one, of a very paltry imagination, which Bossuet did not encourage. What could she do? Nature had denied her wings; she saw plainly that most certainly she would not be able to fly. At any rate, she had no pride; she did not try to conceal the sad condition of her heart; and this humiliating confession escapes her; "I am bursting with jealousy."

What affects us the most is, that after having made the confession, this poor creature, so very gentle, and so very good, sacrificed her own feelings, and became nurse to her who was the object of her jealousy, and then attacked by a dreadful malady. She accompanied her to Paris, shut herself up with her, took care of her, and at last loved her; for the very reason, perhaps, which just before had produced quite the contrary effect—because she was loved by Bossuet.

Sister Cornuau is evidently mistaken in her jealousy; she herself is the person preferred; we see it now by comparing the different correspondence. For her is reserved all his paternal indulgence; for her alone he seems at times to be affected, as much as his ordinary gravity permits. This man, so occupied, finds time to write her nearly two hundred letters; and he is certainly much more firm and austere with the fine lady of whom she is jealous. He becomes short and almost harsh towards the latter, when the business is to answer the rather difficult confidential questions which she perseveres in putting to him. He postpones his answer to an indefinite period ("to my entire leisure"); and till that time, he forbids her to write upon such subjects, otherwise "he will burn her letters without even reading them (24th November, 1691)." He says, somewhere else, very nobly, concerning these delicate things which may trouble the imagination, "that it was necessary, when one was obliged to speak of, and listen to sufferings of this sort, *to be standing with only the point of the foot upon the earth.*" This perfect honesty, which would never understand anything in a bad sense, makes him sometimes forget the existence of evil more than he ought, and renders him rather incautious. Confident also in his age, then very mature, he occasionally allows himself outbursts of mystic love, that were indiscreet before so impassioned a witness as Sister Cornuau. In presence of this simple, submissive, and in every respect inferior person, he considers himself to be alone; and giving free course to the vivacious instinct of poetry that animated him even in his old days, he does not hesitate to make use of the mysterious language of the Song of Solomon. Sometimes it is in order to calm his penitent, and strengthen her chastity, that he employs this ardent language. I dare not copy the letter (innocent, certainly, but so very imprudent) which he writes from his country-house at Germigny (July 10, 1692), and in which he explains the meaning of the Bride's words, "Support me with flowers, because I languish for love." This potion, which is to cure passion by a stronger one, is marvellously calculated to double the evil. What surprises us much more than this imprudence is, that we find frequently in the intimate correspondence of this great adversary of Quietism, the greater part of the sentiments and practical maxims for which the Quietists were reproached. He takes pleasure in developing their favourite text, *Expectans, expectavi.* "The Bride ought not to hurry; she must wait in expectation of what the Bridegroom will do; if, during the expectation, he caresses the soul, and inclines it to caress him, she must yield her heart. The means of the union is the union itself. All the correspondence of the Bride consists in letting the Bridegroom act."

"Jesus is admirable in the chaste embraces with which He honours His Bride and makes her fruitful; all the virtues are the fruits of His chaste embraces" (February 28, 1693),—"A change of life must follow; *but without the soul even thinking of changing itself.*"

This thoroughly Quietist letter is dated May 30 (1696); and eight days after—sad inconsistency!—he writes these unfeeling words about Madame Guyon; "They appear to me resolved to shut her up far away in some good castle," &c.

How is it he does not perceive that in practical questions, far more important than theory, he differs in nothing from those whom he treats so badly? The direction, in Bossuet, as in his adversaries, is the development of the inert and passive part of our nature, *expectans, expectavi.*

For me it is a strange sight to see them all, even in the midst of the middle age, crying out against the mystics, and then falling into mysticism themselves. The declivity must, indeed, be rapid and insurmountable.

In the fourteenth and fifteenth centuries, the profound Rusbrock and the great Gerson imitate precisely those they blame; and in the seventeenth, the Quietists Bona, Fenelon, even Lacombe, Madame Guyon's director, speak severely and harshly of the absolute Quietists: they all point out the abyss, and all fall into it themselves.

No matter who the person may be, there is a logical fatality. The man who, by his character and genius is the farthest removed from passive measures, he who in his writings condemns them the most strongly, even Bossuet, in practice tends towards them, like the others.

What signifies their writing against the theory of Quietism? Quietism is much more a method than a system: a method of drowsiness and indolence which we ever meet with, in one, shape or other, in religious direction. It is useless to recommend activity, like Bossuet, or to permit it, like Fenelon, if, preventing every active exercise of the soul, and holding it, as it were, in leading-strings, you deprive it of the habit, taste, and power of acting.

Is it not then an illusion, Bossuet? if the soul still seems to act, when this activity is no longer its own, but yours. You show me a person who moves and walks; but I see well that this appearance of motion proceeds from your influence over that person, you yourself being, as it were, the principle of action, the cause and reason of living, walking, and moving.

There is always the same sum of action in the total; only, in this dangerous affinity between the director and the person directed, all the action is on the side of the former; he alone remains an active force, a will, a person; he who is directed losing gradually all that constitutes his personality, becomes—what?—a machine.

When Pascal, in his proud contempt for reason, engages us *to become stupid*, and bend within us what he calls the *automaton* and *machine*, he does not see that it will only be an *exchange* of reason. Our reason having herself put on the bit and bridle, that of another man will mount, ride, and guide it at his will, as he would a horse.

If the automaton should still possess some motion, how will they lead it? According to the *probable* opinion, for the *probablism* of the Jesuits reigned in the first half of the century. Later, when its motion ceased, the paralysed age learned from the Quietists that immobility is perfection itself.

The decay and impotency which characterised the latter years of Louis XIV. are rather veiled by a remnant of literary splendour; they are, nevertheless, deeply seated. This was the natural consequence, not only of great efforts which produce exhaustion, but also of the theories of abnegation, impersonality, and systematic nullity, which had always gained ground in this century. By dint of continually repeating that one cannot walk well without being supported by another, a generation arose that no longer walked at all, but boasted of having forgotten what motion was, and gloried in it. Madame Guyon, in speaking of herself, expresses forcibly, in a letter to Bossuet, what was then the general condition: "You say, Monseigneur, there are only four or five persons who are in this difficulty of acting for themselves; but I tell you there are more than a hundred thousand. When you told me to ask and desire, I found myself like a paralytic who is told to walk because *he has legs*: the efforts he makes for that purpose serve only to make him aware of his inability. We say, in common parlance, *every man who has legs ought to walk*: I believe it, and I know it; however, I have legs, but I feel plainly that I cannot make use of them."

CHAPTER X.

MOLINOS' GUIDE;—THE PART PLAYED IN IT BY THE DIRECTOR;—HYPOCRITICAL AUSTERITY;—IMMORAL DOCTRINE.—MOLINOS APPROVED OF AT ROME, 1675.— MOLINOS CONDEMNED AT ROME, 1687.—HIS MANNERS CONFORMABLE TO HIS DOCTRINE.—SPANISH MOLINOSISTS.—MOTHER AGUEDA.

The greatest danger for the poor paralytic, who can no longer move by himself, is, not that he may remain inactive, but that he may become the sport of the active influence of others. The theories which speak the most of immobility are not always disinterested. Be on your guard, and take care.

Molinos' book, with its artful and premeditated composition, has a character entirely its own, which distinguishes it from the natural and inspired writings of the great mystics. The latter, such as Sta. Theresa, often recommend obedience and entire submission to the director, and dissuade from self-confidence. They thus give themselves a guide, but in their enthusiastic efforts they hurry their guide away with them; they think they follow him, but they lead him. The director has nothing else to do with them but to sanction their inspiration.

The originality of Molinos' book is quite the contrary. There, internal activity has actually no longer any existence; no action but what is occasioned by an exterior impulse. *The director* is the pivot of the whole book; he appears every moment, and even when he disappears, we perceive he is close at hand. He is *the guide*, or rather the support, without which the powerless soul could not move a step. He is the ever-present physician, who decides whether the sick patient may taste this or that. Sick? Yes; and seriously ill; since it is necessary that another should, every moment, think, feel, and act for her; in a word, live in her place.

As for the soul, can we say it lives? Is this not rather actual death? The great mystics sought for death, and could not find it: the living activity remained even in the sepulchre. To die, singly, in God, to die with one's own will and energy, this is not dying completely. But slothfully to allow your soul to enter the mad vortex of another soul, and suffer, half-asleep, the strange transformation in which your personality is absorbed in his; this is, indeed, real moral death; we need not look for any other.

"To act, is the deed of the novice; to suffer, is immediate gain; to die, is perfection. Let us go forward in darkness, and we shall go well; the horse that goes round blind-folded grinds corn so much the better. Let us neither think nor read. A *practical* master will tell us, better than any book, what we must do at the very moment. It is a great security to have an experienced guide to govern and direct us, according to his actual intelligence, and prevent our being deceived by the demon or our own senses."[1]

Molinos, in leading us gently by this road, seems to me to know very well whither he is conducting us. I judge so by the infinite precautions he takes to re-assure us; by his crying up everywhere humility, austerity, excessive scrupulousness, and prudence carried to a ridiculous extreme. The saints are not so wise. In a very humble preface, he believes that this little book, devoid of ornament and style, and without a protector, cannot have any success; "he will, no doubt, be criticised; everybody will find him insipid." In the last page, his humility is still greater, he *lays his work prostrate*, and submits it to the correction of the Holy Roman Church.

He gives us to understand, that the real director directs without any inclination for the task: "He is a man who would gladly dispense with the care of souls, who sighs and pants for solitude. He is, especially, very far from wishing to get the direction of women, they being, generally, too little prepared. He must take especial care not to call his penitent *his daughter*; the word is too tender, and God is jealous of it. Self-love united with passion, that hydra-headed monster, sometimes assumes the form of gratitude and filial affection for the confessor. He must not visit his penitents at their homes, not even in cases of sickness, *unless he be called*."

This is, indeed, an astounding severity: these are excessive precautions, unheard of before the days of Molinos! What holy man have we here? It is true, if the director ought not to go of his own accord to visit the patient, he may, *if she call him*. And *I* say, she will call him. With such a direction, is she not always ill, embarrassed, fearful, and too infirm to do anything of herself? She will wish to have him every hour. Every impulse that is not from him might possibly proceed from the devil; even the pang of remorse, that she occasionally feels within her, may be occasioned by the devil's agency.

As soon as he is with her, on the contrary, how tranquil she becomes! How he comforts her with one word! How easily he resolves all her scruples! She is well rewarded for having waited and obeyed, and being ever ready to obey. She now feels that obedience is better than any virtue.

Well! let her only be discreet, and she will be led still further. "She must not, when she sins, be uneasy about it; for should she be grieved at it, it would be a sign that she still possessed a leaven of pride. It is the devil, who, to hinder us in our spiritual path, makes us busy with our backslidings. Would it not be foolish for him who runs to stop when he falls, and weep like a child, instead of pursuing his course? These falls have the excellent effect of preserving us from pride, which is the greatest fall of all. God makes virtues of our vices, and these very vices, by which the devil thought to cast us into the pit, become a ladder to mount to heaven."[2]

This doctrine was well received. Molinos had the tact to publish, at the same time, another book, that might serve as a passport to this, a treatise on *Daily Communion*, directed against the Jansenists and Arnaud's great work. The *Spiritual Guide* was examined with all the favour that Rome could show to the enemy of her enemies. There was scarcely any Religious Order that did not approve of it. The Roman Inquisition gave it three approbations by three of its members, a Jesuit, a Carmelite, and the general of the Franciscans. The Spanish Inquisition approved of it twice;—first, by the general examiner of the order of the Capuchins; and, secondly, by a Trinitarian, the Archbishop of Reggio. It was prefaced with an enthusiastic and extravagant eulogy by the Archbishop of Palermo.

The Quietists must have been at that time very strong in Rome, since one of them, Cardinal Bona, was on the point of being made pope.

The tide turned, contrary to every expectation. The great Gallic tempest of 1682, which, for nearly ten years, interrupted the connection between France and the Holy See, and showed how easily one may dispense with Rome, obliged the pope to raise the moral dignity of the pontificate, by acts of severity. The lash fell especially upon the Jesuits and their friends. Innocent XI. pronounced a solemn condemnation upon the casuists, though rather too late, as these people had been crushed twenty years before by Pascal. But Quietism still flourished: the Franciscans and Jesuits had taken it into favour; the Dominicans were therefore averse to it. Molinos, in his *Manuel*, had considerably reduced the merits of St. Dominic, and pretended that *St. Thomas, when dying, confessed that he had not, up to that time, written anything good.* Accordingly, of all the great Religious Orders, that of the Dominicans was the only one which refused its approbation to Molinos' *Guide*.

The book and its author, examined under this new influence, appeared horribly guilty. The Inquisition of Rome, without taking any notice of the approbations granted twelve years before by their examiners, condemned the *Guide*, together with some propositions not contained in it, but which they extracted from the examination of Molinos, or from his teaching. This one is not the least curious: "God, to humble us, permits, in certain perfect souls (well enlightened and in their lucid state), that the devil should make them commit certain carnal acts. In this case, and in others, which, without the permission of God, would be guilty, there is no sin, because there is no consent. It may happen, that those violent movements, which excite to carnal acts, may take place in two persons, a man and a woman, at the same moment."[3]

This case happened to Molinos himself, and much too often. He underwent a public penance, humbled himself for his morals, and did not defend his doctrine: this saved him. The inquisitors, who had formerly approved of him, must have been themselves much embarrassed about this trial. He was treated with leniency, and only imprisoned, whilst two of his disciples, who had only faithfully applied his doctrine, were burned alive without pity. One was a curate of Dijon, the other a priest of Tudela in Navarre.

How can we be surprised that such a theory should have had such results in morals? It would be much more astonishing if it had not. Besides, these immoral results do not proceed exclusively from Molinosism, a doctrine at once imprudent and too evident, and which they would take good care not to profess. They spring naturally from every practical direction that lulls the will, taking from the person this natural guardian, and exposing him thus prostrate to the mercy of him who watches over the sick couch. The tale told more than once by the middle ages, and which casuists have examined so coldly, the violation of the dead, we here meet with again. The person is left as defenceless by the death of the will, as by physical death.

The Archbishop of Palermo, in his Pindaric eulogy of the *Spiritual Guide*, says that this admirable book is most especially suitable to the *direction of nuns*. The advice was understood, and turned to account, especially in Spain. From that saying of Molinos, "That sins, being an occasion of humility, serve as a ladder to mount to heaven," the Molinosists drew this consequence—the more we sin the higher we ascend.

There was among the Carmelites of Lerma a holy woman, Mother Agueda, esteemed as a saint. People went to her from all the neighbouring provinces, to get her to cure the sick. A convent was founded on the spot that had been so fortunate as to give her birth. There, in the church, they adored her portrait placed within the choir; and there she cured those who were brought to her, by applying to them certain miraculous stones which she brought forth, as they said, with pains similar to those of childbirth. This miracle lasted twenty years. At last the report spread that these confinements were but too true, and that she was really delivered. The inquisition of Logrogno having made a visit to the convent, arrested Mother Agueda, and questioned the other nuns, among whom was the young niece of the Saint, Donna Vincenta. The latter confessed, without any prevarication, the commerce that her aunt, herself, and the others had had with the provincial of the Carmelites, the prior of Lerma, and other friars of the first rank. The Saint had been confined five times, and her niece showed the place where the children had been killed and buried the moment they were born. They found the skeletons.

What is not less horrible is, that this young nun, only nine years of age, a dutiful child, immured by her aunt for this strange life, and having no other education, firmly believed that this was really the devout life, perfection, and sanctity, and followed this path in full confidence, upon the faith of her confessors.

The grand doctor of these nuns was the provincial of the Carmelites, Jean de la Vega. He had written the life of the Saint, and arranged her miracles; and he it was who had the skill to have her glorified, and her festival observed, though she was still alive. He himself was considered almost a saint by the vulgar. The monks said everywhere that, since the blessed Jean de la Croix, Spain had not seen a man so austere and penitent. According to their custom of designating illustrious doctors by a titular name (such as Angelic, Seraphic, &c.), he was called the Ecstatic. Being much stronger than the saint, he resisted the torture, where as she died in it: he confessed nothing, except that he had received the money for eleven thousand eight hundred masses that he had not said; and he got off with being banished to the convent of Duruelo.

[1] Molinos, Guida Spirituale (Venetia, 1685), pp. 86, 161.

[2] "Scala per salire al cielo,"—*Guida*, p. 138. lib. ii. ch. 18.

[3] Condemned articles, pp. 41, 42., Lat. transl. (Lipsiæ, 1687.)

CHAPTER XI.

NO MORE SYSTEMS;—AN EMBLEM.—BLOOD.—SEX.—THE IMMACULATE WOMAN.—THE SACRED HEART.—MARIE ALACOQUE.—DOUBLE MEANING OF SACRED HEART.— THE SEVENTEENTH CENTURY IS THE AGE OF DOUBLE MEANING.—CHIMERICAL POLICY OF THE JESUITS.— FATHER COLOMBIERE AND MARIE ALACOQUE, 1675.— ENGLAND;—PAPIST CONSPIRACY.—FIRST ALTAR OF THE SACRED HEART, 1685.—RUIN OF THE GALLICANS, 1693;— OF THE QUIETISTS, 1698;—OF PORT ROYAL, 1709.— THEOLOGY ANNIHILATED IN THE EIGHTEENTH CENTURY.—MATERIALITY OF THE SACRED HEART.— JESUITICAL ART.

Quietism, so accused of being obscure, was but too evident. It formed into a system, and established frankly, as supreme perfection, that state of immobility and impotency which the soul reaches at last, when it surrenders its activity.

Was it not simplicity itself to prescribe in set terms this lethargic doctrine, and give out noisily a theory of sleep? "Do not speak so loud if you want to make people doze?" This is what the theologians, men of business, instinctively perceived; they cared little for theology, and only wanted results.

We must do the Jesuits the justice to confess that they were disinterested enough in speculative opinions. We have seen how, since Pascal, they themselves wrote against their own casuistry. Since then they had tried Quietism: at one time they let Fenelon believe they would support him. But as soon as Louis XIV. had declared himself, "they ducked like divers," preached against their friend, and discovered forty errors in the *Maxims of Saints*.

They had never well succeeded as theologians. Silence suited them better than all their systems. They had got it imposed by the pope upon the Dominicans, in the very beginning of the century, and afterwards upon the Jansenists. Since then their affairs went on better. It was precisely at the time they ceased writing, that they obtained for the sick king the power of disposing of benefices (1687), and thus, to the great surprise of the

Gallicans, who had thought them conquered, they became the kings of the clergy of France.

Now, no more ideas, no more systems; they had grown tired of them. Long ago we mentioned the prevailing lassitude. Besides, there is, we must confess, in the long lives of men, states, and religions; there is, I say, a time when, having run from project to project, and from dream to dream, every idea is hated. In these profoundly material moments, everything is rejected that is not tangible. Do people then become positive? No. But they do not return any more to the poetical symbols which in their youth they had adored. The old doter, in his second childhood, makes for himself some idol, some palpable, tangible god, and the coarser it is, the better he succeeds.

This explains the prodigious success with which the Jesuits in this age of lassitude spread, and caused to be accepted, a new object of worship, both very carnal and very material—the Heart of Jesus, either shown through the wound in His partly opened breast, or as plucked out and bloody.

Nearly the same thing had happened in the decrepitude of paganism. Religion had taken refuge in the sacrifice of bulls, the sanguinary Mithraic expiation—the worship of blood.

At the grand festival of the *Sacred Heart* which the Jesuits gave in the last century, in the Coliseum of Rome, they struck a medal with this motto, worthy of the solemnity, "He gave Himself to the people to eat, in the amphitheatre of Titus:"[1] instead of a system, it was an emblem, a dumb sign. What triumph for the friends of obscurity and equivocation! no equivocation of language can equal a material object, which may be interpreted in a thousand ways, for rendering ideas undecided and confused. The old Christian symbols, so often translated, and so variously interpreted, present to the mind, at first sight, too distinct a meaning. They are austere symbols of death and mortification. The new one was far more obscure. This emblem, bloody it is true, but carnal and impassioned, speaks much less of death than of life. The heart palpitates, the blood streams, and yet it is a living man who, showing his wound with his own hand, beckons to you to come and fathom his half-opened breast.

The heart! That word has always been powerful; the heart, being the organ of the affections, expresses them in its own manner, swollen and heaving with sighs. The life of the heart, strong and confused, comprehends and mingles every kind of love. Such a sentence is wonderfully adapted to language of double meaning.

And who will understand it best? Women. With them the life of the heart is everything. This organ, being the passage of the blood, and strongly influenced by the revolutions of the blood, is not less predominant in woman than her very sex.

The heart has been, now nearly two hundred years, the grand basis of modern devotion; as sex, or a strange question that related to it, had, for two hundred before, occupied the minds of the middle ages.

Strange! in that spiritual period, a long discussion, both public and solemn, took place throughout Europe, both in the schools and in the churches, upon an anatomical subject, of which one would not dare to speak in our days, except in the school of medicine! What was this subject? Conception. Only imagine all these monks, people sworn to celibacy, both Dominicans and Franciscans, boldly attacking the question, teaching it to all, preaching anatomy to children and little girls, filling their minds with their sex and its most secret mystery.

The heart, a more noble organ, had the advantage of furnishing a number of dubious though decent expressions, a whole language of equivocal tenderness which did not cause a blush, and facilitated the intrigue of devout gallantry.

In the very beginning of the seventeenth century, the directors and confessors find a very convenient text in *The Sacred Heart*. But women take it quite differently, and in a serious sense: they grow warm and impassioned, and have visions. The Virgin appears to a country girl of Normandy, and orders her to adore the heart of Mary. The Visitandines called themselves the daughters of the *Heart of Jesus*. Jesus does not fail to appear to a Visitandine, Mademoiselle Marie Alacoque, and shows her His heart and wound.

She was a strong girl, and of a sanguine temperament, whom they were obliged to bleed constantly. She had entered the convent in her twenty-fourth year, with her passions entire; her infancy had not been miserably nipped in the bud, as it often happens to those who are immured at an early age. Her devotion was, from the very first, a violent love, that wished to suffer for the object loved. Having heard that Madame de Chantal had printed the name of Jesus on her breast with a hot iron, she did the same. The Lover was not insensible to this, and ever after visited her. It was with the knowledge, and under the direction of a skilful superior, that Marie Alacoque made this intimate connection with the Divine Bridegroom. She celebrated her espousals with Him; and a regular contract was drawn up by the superior, which Marie Alacoque signed with her blood. One day, when, according to her biographer, she had cleaned with her tongue the lips of a sick person, Jesus was so satisfied with her, that He permitted her to fix her lips to one of His Divine wounds.

There was nothing in this relating to theology. It was merely a subject of physiology and medicine. Mademoiselle Alacoque was a girl of an ardent disposition, which was heightened by celibacy. She was by no means a mystic in the proper sense of the word. Happier far than Madame Guyon, who did not see what she loved, she saw and touched the body of the Divine Lover. The heart He showed her in His unseamed breast was a bloody intestine. The extremely sanguine plethory from which she was suffering, and which frequent bleeding could not relieve, filled her imagination with these visions of blood.

The Jesuits, who were great propagators of the new devotion, took good care not to explain precisely whether homage was to be paid to the symbolical heart and celestial love, or whether the heart of flesh was to be the object of adoration. When pressed to explain themselves, their answers depended on persons, times, and places. Their Father Galiffet made, at the same time, two contradictory replies: in Rome he said it was the symbolical heart; and in Paris he said in print that there was no metaphor, that they honoured the flesh itself.

This equivocation was a source of wealth. In less than forty years four hundred and twenty-eight brotherhoods of the Sacred Heart were formed in France.

I cannot help pausing a moment, to admire how Equivocation triumphed throughout this age.

On whatever side I turn my eyes, I find it everywhere, both in things and persons. It sits upon the throne in the person of Madame de Maintenon. Is this person a queen who is seated by the king's side, and before whom princesses are standing—or is she not? The equivocal is also near the throne in the person of the humble Père la Chaise, the real king of the clergy of France, who from a garret at Versailles distributes the benefices. And do our loyal Galileans and the scrupulous Jansenists abstain from the equivocal? Obedient, yet rebellious, preparing war though kneeling, they kiss the foot of the pope, while wishing to tie his hands; they spoil the best reasons by their *distinguo* and evasions. Indeed, when I put in opposition to the sixteenth and eighteenth centuries this Janus of the seventeenth, the two others appear to me as honest centuries, or, at the very least, sincere in good and in evil. But what falsehood and ugliness is concealed under the majestic harmony of the seventeenth! Everything is softened and shaded in the form, but the bottom is often the worse for it. Instead of the local inquisitions, you have the police of the Jesuits, armed with the king's authority. In place of a Saint Bartholomew, you have the long, the immense religious revolution, called the Revocation of the Edict of Nantes, that cruel comedy of forced conversion; then the unheard-of tragedy of a proscription organised by all the bureaucratical and military means of a modern government!—Bossuet sings the triumph; and deceit, lying, and misery reign everywhere! Deceit in politics; local life destroyed without creating any central life. Deceit in morals: this polished court, this world of polite people receives an unexpected lesson from the *chamber of poisons*: the king suppresses the trial, fearing to find every one guilty!—And can devotion be real with such morals?—If you reproach the sixteenth century with its violent fanaticism, if the eighteenth appear to you cynical and devoid of human respect, confess at least also that lying, deceit, and hypocrisy are the predominant features of the seventeenth. That great historian Molière has painted the portrait of this century, and found its name—Tartuffe.

I return to the Sacred Heart, which, in truth, I have not quitted, since it is during this period the illustrious and predominant example of the success of the equivocal. The Jesuits who, in general, have invented little, did not make the discovery, but they perceived very plainly the profit they might derive from it. We have seen how they gradually made themselves masters of the convents of women, though professing all the time to be strangers to them. The Visitation, especially, was under their influence. The superior of Marie Alacoque, who had her confidence, and directed her connection with Jesus Christ, gave timely notice to Père La Chaise.

The thing happened just in time. The Jesuits sadly wanted some popular machine to set in motion, for the profit of their policy. It was the moment when they thought, at least they told the king so, that England, sold by Charles II., would, in a short time, be entirely converted. Intrigue, money, women, everything was turned to account, to bring it about. To King Charles they gave mistresses, and to his brother, confessors. The Jesuits, who, with all their tricks, are often chimerical, thought that by gaining over five or six lords, they would change all that Protestant mass, which is Protestant not only by belief, but also by interest, habit, and manner of living; Protestant to the core, and with English tenacity.

See then these famous politicians, gliding as stealthily as wolves, and fancying they will carry everything by surprise. An essential point for them was to place with James, the king's brother, a secret preacher, who, in his private chapel, might work silently, and try his hand at a few conversions. To act the part of a converter, they required a man who was not only captivating, but especially ardent and fanatical; such men were scarce. The latter qualifications were deficient in the young man whom Père La Chaise had in view. This was a Father La Colombière, who taught rhetoric in their college at Lyons; he was an agreeable preacher, an elegant writer, much esteemed by Patru, mild, docile, and a good sort of man. The only thing that was wanting was a little madness. To inoculate him with this, they introduced him to Mademoiselle Alacoque: he was sent to Paray-le-Monial, where she resided, as confessor extraordinary of the Visitandines (1675). He was in his thirty-fourth year, and she in her twenty-eighth. Having been well prepared by her superior, she immediately saw in him the great servant of God, whom her visions had revealed to her, and the very same day she perceived in the ardent heart of Jesus her own heart united to the Jesuit's.

La Colombière, being of a mild and feeble nature, was hurried away unresistingly into this ardent vortex of passion and fanaticism. He was kept for a year and a half in this spiritual furnace; he was then snatched away from Paray, and hurled red-hot into England. They were, however, still mistrustful of him, fearing he might cool, and sent him, from time to time, a few ardent and inspired lines: Marie Alacoque dictated, and the superior was her amanuensis.

He remained thus two years with the Duchess of York in London, so well concealed and shut up, that he did not even see the town. They brought to him, mysteriously, a few lords, who thought it advantageous to be converted to the religion of the heir presumptive. England having at last discovered the Papal conspiracy, La Colombière was accused, brought before Parliament, and embarked for France, where he arrived ill; and though his superior sent him to Paray to see whether the nun could revive him, he died there of a fever.

However little inclined people may be to believe that great results are brought about by trifling causes, they are obliged, however, to confess that this miserable intrigue had an incalculable effect upon France and the world. They wanted to gain England, and they presented themselves to her, not in the persons of the Gallicans, whom she respected, but in those of the Jesuits, whom she had always abhorred. At the very moment when Catholicism ought, in prudence at least, to have discarded the idolatries with which the Protestants reproached it, they published a new one, and the most offensive of all, the carnal and sensual devotion of the Sacred Heart. To mingle horror with ridicule, it was in 1685, the sad and lamentable year of the Revocation of the Edict of Nantes, that Marie Alacoque raised the first of those altars which overspread the whole of France. We know how England, confirmed in her Protestantism and horror of Rome by the Jesuits, took to herself a Dutch king, carried away Holland in her movement, and by this conjunction of the two maritime powers obtained the dominion of the seas.

The Jesuits may boast that they have been the means of setting Protestantism in England upon a very solid foundation. All the Father Mathews in the world will never be able to remove it.

Their political work, as we have seen, is important: it ended in marrying England to Holland—a marriage nearly fatal to France.

And what was their religious work among us in the old days of Louis XIV.? What was the last use made of the omnipotent sway of the La Chaises and the Telliers? We well know: the destruction of Port-Royal, a military expedition to carry off fifteen old women, the dead dragged from their graves, and sacrilege committed by the hands of authority. This authority expiring in the terrible year 1709, which seemed to carry off at one blow the king and the kingdom, was employed by them, in all haste, to destroy their enemies.

Port-Royal came to an end in 1709, Quietism had finished in 1698, and Gallicanism itself, the great religion of the throne, had been placed at the feet of the pope by the king in 1693. Behold Bossuet laid in the tomb by the side of Fenelon, and the latter next to Arnaud. The conquerors and the conquered repose in a common nullity.

The emblem prevailing, and being substituted for every system, people felt less and less the need of analysing, explaining, and thinking; and they were glad of it. The explanation the most favourable to authority is still a giving of accounts, that is to say, a homage paid to the liberty of the mind. But in the shadow of an obscure emblem one may henceforth without shaping any theory, or allowing any advantage to be taken, apply indifferently the practice of all the various theories that had been abandoned, and follow them alternately or conjointly, according to the interest of the day.

Wise policy, excellent wisdom, with which they cover their nothingness! Having dispensed with reasoning for others, they lose the faculty of reasoning altogether, and, in the hour of danger, they find themselves disarmed. This is what happened to them in the eighteenth century. The terribly learned contest that then took place found them mute. Voltaire let fly a hundred thousand arrows against them, without awakening them. Rousseau pressed and crushed them without getting one word out of them.

Who then could answer? Theology was no longer known to the theologians. The persecutors of the Jansenists mingle in their books published in the name of Marie Alacoque, both Jansenist and Molinist opinions, and without being aware of it. They composed in 1708 the manual which has since become the basis of instruction adopted in our seminaries; and this manual contains the entirely new doctrine, that on every Papal decision Jesus Christ *inspires* the pope to decide, and the bishops to obey: every thing is an oracle and a miracle in this clownish system. Reason is decidedly rooted out of theology.

From that time there is very little of a dogmatical character, and still less of sacred history; an instruction which would be void, if ancient casuistry did not assist in filling up the vacuum with immoral subtilties.

The only part of mankind to whom they have addressed themselves for a long time, namely, women, is the world of sensibility. They do not ask for science; they wish for impressions rather than ideas. The less they are busied about ideas the easier it is to keep them ignorant of outward events, and make them strangers to the progress of time.

When they maintain that holiness consists in sacrificing the mind, the more material the worship, the more it serves to attain that end; the more the mind is degraded the holier it becomes. To couple salvation with the exercise of moral virtues, would be to require the exercise of reason. But what do they want with virtue? Wear this medal: "*It will blot out your iniquities.*" Reason would still have a share in religion, if, as reason teaches us, it was necessary for salvation absolutely to love God. Marie Alacoque has seen that it was sufficient *not to hate Him*; and those who are devoted to the Sacred Heart are saved unconditionally.

When the Jesuits were suppressed, they had in their hands no other religious means than this paganism, and in it they placed all their hope of coming to life again. They had engravings made, to which they added the motto, "I will give them the shield of my heart."

The popes, who, at first, were uneasy about the weak point which such a materialism would offer to the attacks of the philosophers, have found out in our time that it is very useful to them, being addressed to a class of people who seldom read the philosophers, and who, though devout, are nevertheless material. They have therefore preserved the precious equivocation of the ideal and the carnal heart, and forbidden any explanation as to whether the words "*Sacred Heart*" designated the love of God for man, or some bit of bleeding flesh. By reducing the thing to the idea, the impassioned attraction in which its success consisted would be taken from it.

Even in the last century, some bishops had gone farther, declaring that *flesh* was here the *principal* object; and they had placed this flesh in certain hymns, after the Trinity, as a fourth person. Priests, women, and young girls have all since then vied with one another in this devotion. I have before me a manual, much used in country places, in which they teach the persons of their community, who pray for one another, how they join hearts, and how these hearts, once united, "ought to desire to enter into the opening of the heart of Jesus, and be incessantly sinking into that amorous wound."

The brotherhood, in their manuals, have occasionally found it gallant to put the heart of Mary above that of Jesus (see that of Nantes, 1769). In their engravings she is generally younger than her Son, being, for instance, about twenty, whereas he is thirty years old, so that, at first sight, He seems to be rather her husband or lover than her Son.

This very year I saw at Rouen, in the Church of St. Ouen, in the Chapel of the *Sacred Heart*, a pen-and-ink drawing, by young ladies, having the written approbation of the ecclesiastical authorities, in which Jesus is represented on His knees before the Virgin, who is also kneeling.

The most violent satire against the Jesuits is what they have made themselves—their art, the pictures and statues they have inspired. They are at once characterised by the severe sentence of Poussin, whose Christ did not appear to them pretty enough: "We cannot imagine a Christ with His head on one side, or like Father Donillet's." Yet Poussin saw the best days of the Jesuit art: what would he have said if he had seen what followed? all that decrepid coquetry that thinks it smiles whilst it grimaces, those ridiculous glances, dying eyes, and such like deformities. The worst is, they who think only of the flesh know no longer how to represent it. As the thought grows more and more material and insipid, the form becomes defaced, degraded from picture to picture, ignoble, foppish, affected, heavy, dull—that is to say, shapeless.[2]

We may judge of men by the art they inspire; and I confess it is no easy task to augur favourably of the souls of those who inspire this art, and recommend these engravings, hanging them up in their churches and distributing them by thousands and millions. Such taste is an ominous sign. Many immoral people still possess a sentiment of elegance. But willingly to take to the ignoble and false discovers a sad degradation of the soul.

An undeniable truth is here made manifest; which is, that art is the only thing inaccessible to falsehood. Being the offspring of the heart and natural inspiration, it cannot be allied to what is false, it will not be violated; it protests, and if the false triumphs, it dies. All the rest may be aped and acted. They very well managed to make a theology in the sixteenth and a morality in the seventeenth century; but never could they form an art. They can ape the holy and the just; but how can they mimic the beautiful?— Thou art ugly, poor Tartuffe, and ugly shalt thou remain: it is thy token. What! you reach the beautiful, or ever lay a finger upon it? This would be impious beyond all impiety!—The beautiful is the face of God!

[1] In 1771. On Sacred Hearts (by Tabaraud), p. 82.

[2] In 1834, being busy with Christian iconography, I looked over the collections of the portraits of Christ in the Royal Library. Those published within the last thirty years are the most humiliating I have ever seen, both for art and human nature. Every man (whether a philosopher or a believer) who retains any sentiment of religion will be disgusted with them. Every impropriety, every sensuality and low passion is there: the childish, dandified seminarist, the licentious priest, the fat curate who looks like *Maingrat*, &c. The engraving is as good as the drawing—a skewer and the snuff of a tallow candle.

PART II.

ON DIRECTION IN GENERAL, AND ESPECIALLY IN THE NINETEENTH CENTURY.

CHAPTER I.

RESEMBLANCES AND DIFFERENCES BETWEEN THE SEVENTEENTH AND NINETEENTH CENTURIES.— CHRISTIAN ART.—IT IS WE WHO HAVE RESTORED THE CHURCH.—WHAT IT ADDS TO THE POWER OF THE PRIEST.—THE CONFESSIONAL.

There are two objections to be made against all that I have said, and I will state them:—

First. "The examples are taken from the seventeenth century, at a time when the direction was influenced by theological questions, which now no longer occupy either the world or the Church; for instance, the question of grace and free-will, and that of Quietism or repose in love." But this I have already answered. Such questions are obsolete, dead, if you will, as theories; but, in the spirit and practical method which emanate from these theories, they are, and ever will be, living. There are no longer to be found speculative people, simple enough to trace out expressly a doctrine of lethargy and moral annihilation; but there will always be found enough quacks to practice quietly this lethargic art. If this be not clear enough, I will, in a moment, make it clearer than some people would desire.

Secondly. "Are the examples you have shown from the books and letters of the great men of the famous age sufficiently conclusive for our own time? Might not those profound and subtle men of genius, who dived so deeply into the science of directing souls, have entered into refinements, of which the common herd of confessors and directors cannot now conceive any idea? Can you fear anything of the sort from the poor simple priests whom we have now? Pray where are our St. François de Sales, our Bossuets, and our Fenelons? Do you not see that not only the clergy no longer possess such men, but that they have degenerated generally, and as a class. The great majority of the priests are of rustic families. The peasant, even when he is not poor, finds it convenient to lighten the expenses of his family, by placing his son in the seminary. To nursery education, that which we receive from our parents before any other, they are total strangers. The seminary by no means repairs this inconvenience of origin and former condition. If we judge by those who come from the hands of the Sulpicians, Lazarists, &c., we shall be inclined to believe that there has been a deep plan laid among the upper leaders, to form none but indifferent priests, who would be so much the more dependent, and blind to the influence exercised over them contrary to their real interests. What then do you fear? Is not this intellectual degradation of the clergy sufficiently comforting? How could such men follow, in the confession and direction, the learned tactics of the priests of former ages? The dangers you point out are imaginary."

To this it is easy to answer:—

Mental distinction and good education are not so necessary, as is generally thought, for enslaving souls that are willing to be ruled. Authority, character, position, and costume fortify the *Priest*, and make good in him what was wanting in the *Man*. He gains his ascendency less by his skill than by time and perseverance. If his mind is but little cultivated, it is also less taken up with a variety of new ideas, which incessantly come crowding upon us moderns, amusing and fatiguing us. With fewer ideas, views, and projects, but with an interest, an aim, and ever the same end invariably kept in view—this is the way to succeed.

Must we take it for granted, because you are clownish, you are less cunning on that account? Peasants are circumspect, often full of cunning, and endued with an indefatigable constancy in following up any petty interest. How many long years, what different means, and often indirect ones, will such a one employ, in order to add two feet of land to his field. Do you think that his son, *Monsieur le Curé*, will be less patient or less ardent in his endeavours to get possession of a soul, to govern this woman, or to enter that family?

These peasant families have often much vigour, a certain sap, belonging to the blood and constitution, which either gives wit, or supplies the place of it. Those in the South especially, where the clergy raise their principal recruits, furnish them with intrepid speakers, who do not need to know anything; and who, by their very ignorance, are, perhaps, only in a more direct communication with the simple persons, to whom they address themselves. They speak out loudly, with energy and assurance; educated persons would be more reserved, and less proper to fascinate the weak; they would not dare to attempt so audaciously a clownish *Mesmerism* in spiritual things.

In this, I must confess, there is a serious difference between our own century and the seventeenth, when the clergy of all parties were so learned. That culture, those vast studies, that great theological and literary activity were, for the priest of that time, the most powerful diversion in the midst of temptations. Science, or, at the very least, controversy and disputation, created for him, in a position that was often very worldly, a sort of solitude, an *alibi*, as one may say, that effectually preserved him. But ours, who have nothing of the sort, who, moreover, spring from a hardy and material race, and do not know how to employ this embarrassing vigour, must indeed require a fund of virtue!

The great men from whom we have drawn our examples, had a wonderful defence against spiritual and carnal desires; better than a defence, they had wings that raised them from the earth, at the critical moment, above temptation. By these wings, I mean the love of God, the love of genius for itself, its natural effort to remain on high and ascend, its abhorrence of degradation.

Being chiefs of the clergy of France, the only clergy then flourishing, and responsible to the world for whatever subsisted by their faith, they kept their hearts exalted to the level of the great part they had to perform. One thought was the guardian of their lives—a thought which they repressed, but which did not the less sustain them in delicate trials: it was this, "In them resided the Church."

Their great experience of the world and domestic life, their tact and skilful management of men and things, far from weakening morality, as one might believe, rather defended it in them, enabling them to perceive, and have a presentiment of perils, to see the enemy coming, not to allow him the advantage of unexpected attacks; or, at least, to know how to elude him.

We have seen how Bossuet stopped the soft confidence of a weak nun at the very first word. The little we have said of Fenelon's *direction* shows sufficiently how the dangerous director evaded the dangers.

Those eminently spiritual persons could keep up for years between heaven and earth this tender dialectic of the love of God. But is it the same in these days with men who have no wings, who crawl and cannot fly? Incapable of those ingenious turnings and windings by which passion went on sportively, and eluding itself, do they not run the risk of stumbling at the first step?

I know well that this absence of early education, and vulgarity or clownishness, may often put an insurmountable barrier between priests and well-bred women. Many things, however, that would not be tolerated in another man are reckoned in them as merits. Stiffness is austerity, and awkwardness is accounted the simplicity of a saint, who has ever lived in a desert. They are measured by a different and more indulgent rule than the laity. The priest takes advantage of everything that is calculated to make him be considered as a man apart, of his dress, his position, his mysterious church, that invests the most vulgar with a poetical gleam.

Who gave them this last advantage? Ourselves. We, who have reinstated, rebuilt, as one may say, those very churches they had disregarded. The priests were building up their Saint-Sulpices, and other heaps of stones, when the laity retrieved Nôtre-Dame and Saint Ouen. We pointed out to them the Christian spirit of these living stones,[1] but they did not see it; we taught it them, but they could not understand. And how long did the misconception last? Not less than forty years, ever since the appearance of the *Génie de Christianisme*. The priests would not believe us, when we explained to them this sublime edifice; they did not recognise it; but who can wonder? It belongs only to those who understood it.

At length, however, they have changed their opinion. They have found it to be political and clever to speak as we do, and extol Christian architecture. They have decked themselves out with their churches, again invested themselves with this glorious cloak, and assumed in them a triumphant posture. The crowd comes, looks, and admires. Truly, if we are to judge of a well-dressed man by his coat, he who is invested with the splendour of a Nôtre-Dame of Paris, or a Cologne cathedral, is apparently the giant of the spiritual world. Alexander, on his departure from India, wishing to deceive posterity as to the size of his Macedonians, had a camp traced out on the ground in which a space of ten feet was allotted to each of his soldiers. What an immense place is this church, and what an immense host must inhabit this wonderful dwelling! Optical delusion adds still more to the effect. Every proportion changes. The eye is deceived and deceives itself, at the same time, with these sublime lights and deepening shades, all calculated to increase the illusion. The man whom in the street you judged, by his surly look, to be a village schoolmaster, is here a prophet. He is transformed by this majestic framework; his heaviness becomes strength and majesty; his voice has formidable echoes. Women and children tremble and are afraid.

When a woman returns home, she finds everything prosy and paltry. Had she even Pierre Corneille for a husband, she would think him pitiful, if he lived in the dull house they still show us. Intellectual grandeur in a low apartment does not affect her. The comparison makes her sad, bitterly quiet. The husband puts up with it, and smiles, or pretends to do so; "Her director has turned her brain," says he aloud, and adds, aside, "After all, she only sees him at church." But what place, I ask, is more powerful over the imagination, richer in illusions, and more fascinating than the church? It is precisely the church that ennobles, raises, exaggerates, and sheds a poetical ray upon this otherwise vulgar man.

Do you see that solemn figure, adorned with all the gold and purple of his pontifical dress, ascending with the thought, the prayer of a multitude of ten thousand men, the triumphal steps in the choir of St. Denis? Do you see him still, above all that kneeling mass, hovering as high as the vaulted roofs, his head reaching the capitals, and lost among the winged heads of the angels, whence he hurls his thunder? Well, it is the same man, this terrible archangel himself, who presently descends for her, and now, mild and gentle, goes yonder into that dark chapel, to listen to her in the languid hours of the afternoon! Delightful hour of tumultuous, but tender sensations! (Why does the heart palpitate so strongly here?) How dark the church becomes! Yet it is not late. The great rose-window over the portal glitters with the setting sun. But it is quite another thing in the choir; dark shadows envelope it, and beyond is obscurity. One thing astounds and almost frightens us, however far we may be, which is the mysterious old painted glass at the farthest end of the church, on which the design is no longer distinguishable, twinkling in the shade, like an illegible magic scroll of unknown characters. The chapel is not less dark on that account; you can no longer discern the ornaments and delicate moulding entwined in the vaulted roof; the shadow deepening blends and confounds the outlines. But, as if this chapel were not yet dark enough, it contains, in a retired corner, a narrow recess of dark oak, where that man, all emotion, and that trembling woman, so close to each other, are whispering together about the love of God.

[1] See my History of France (1833), the last chapter of Vol. II., and particularly the last ten pages. In this same volume I have made a serious mistake which I wish to rectify. In speaking of ecclesiastical celibacy (temp. Gregory VII.), I have said that married men could never have raised those sublime monuments, the spire of Strasbourg, &c. I find, on the contrary, that the architects of the Gothic churches were laymen, and generally married. Erwin de Steinbach, who built Strasbourg, had a celebrated daughter, Sabina, who was herself an artist.

CHAPTER II.

CONFESSION.—PRESENT EDUCATION OF THE YOUNG CONFESSOR.—THE CONFESSOR IN THE MIDDLE AGES:—FIRST, BELIEVED; SECONDLY, MORTIFIED HIMSELF; THIRDLY, WAS SUPERIOR BY CULTURE; FOURTHLY, USED TO INTERROGATE LESS.—THE CASUISTS WROTE FOR THEIR TIME.—THE DANGERS OF THE YOUNG CONFESSOR.—HOW HE STRENGTHENS HIS TOTTERING POSITION.

A worthy parish priest has often told me that the sore part of his profession, that which filled him with despair, and his life with torment, was the *Confessional*.

The studies, with which they prepare for it in the seminaries, are such as entirely ruin the disposition, weaken the body, and enervate and defile the soul.

Lay education, without making any pretension to an extraordinary degree of purity, and though the pupils it forms will, one day, enjoy public life, takes, however, especial care to keep from the eyes of youth the glowing descriptions that excite the passions.

Ecclesiastical education, on the contrary, which pretends to form men superior to man, pure virgin minds, angels, fixes precisely the attention of its pupils upon things that are to be for ever forbidden them, and gives them for subjects of study terrible temptations, such as would make all the saints run the risk of damnation. Their printed books have been quoted, but not so their copy-books, by which they complete the two last years of seminary education. These copy-books contain things that the most audacious have never dared to publish.

I dare not quote here what has been revealed to me about this idiotic education by those who have been its martyrs, and narrowly escaped destruction from it. No one can imagine the condition of a poor young man, still a believer, and very sincere, struggling between the terrors and temptations with which they surround him, at pleasure, with two unknown subjects, either one of which might drive him mad, *Woman! Hell!*—and yet obliged to look incessantly at the abyss, blinded, through these impure books, with his sanguine youthful constitution.

This surprising imprudence proceeded originally from the very scholastic supposition, that the body and soul could be perfectly well kept apart. They had imagined they could lead them like two coursers of different tempers, the one to the right and the other to the left. They did not reflect that, in this case, man would be in the predicament of the chariot sculptured upon the tablet of the Louvre, which, pulled both ways, must inevitably be dashed to pieces.

However different these two substances may be in nature, it is but too manifest that they are mingled in action. Not a motion of the soul but acts upon the body, which re-acts in the same manner. The most cruel discipline inflicted upon the body will destroy it rather than prevent its action upon the soul. To believe that a vow, a few prayers, and a black robe, will deliver you from the flesh, and make you a pure spirit—is perfect childishness.

They will refer me to the middle ages, and to the multitudes who have lived mortified lives.

For this I have not one answer, but twenty, which admit of no reply. It is too easy to show that priests in general, and especially the confessor, were then totally different from what they have been for the two last centuries.

I. The first answer will seem, perhaps, harsh—*Then the priest believed.* "What! the priest no longer believes? Do you mean to say that in speaking of his faith with so much energy, he is a hypocrite and a liar?" No, I will allow him to be sincere. But there are two manners of believing, there are many degrees in faith. We are told that Lope de Vega (who, as it is known, was a priest) could not officiate: at the moment of the sacrifice, his fancy pictured the Passion too strongly, he would burst into tears and faint. Compare this with the coquettish pantomine of the Jesuit, who acts mass at Fribourg, or with the prelate whom I have seen at the altar showing to advantage his delicate small hand. The priest believed, and *his penitent believed.* Unheard-of terrors, miracles, devils, and hell, filled the church. The motto, "God hears you," was engraven not only in the wood, but in the heart. It was not a plank that partitioned off the confessional, but the sword of the archangel, the thought of the last judgment.

II. If the priest spoke in the name of the *spirit*, he was partly justified in doing so, having purchased spiritual power by the *suicide of the body.* His long prayers at night would have sufficed to wear him out; but they found more direct means in excessive fasts. Fasting was the diet of those poor schools of Beggars and Cappets, whose scanty meal was composed of arguments. Half dead before the age of manhood, they cooled their blood with herbs producing a deadly chill, and exhausted it by frequent bleedings.

The number of bleedings, to which the monks had to submit, was provided in their rules. Their stomachs were soon destroyed, and their strength impaired. Bernard and Theresa were weakened by continual vomitings, even the sense of taste was lost: the Saint, says his biographer, took blood for butter. *Mortification* was not then an idle word, it was not a separation of the body and soul, but a genuine and honest suppression of the body.

III. The priest believed himself to be, in this sense, the man of the spirit, and he really was so, by the *superiority of culture. He* knew everything, the layman nothing. Even when the priest was young, he was truly the father, the other the child. In our days it is just the contrary; the layman, in cities at least, is generally more learned than the priest. Even the peasant, if he be a father of a family, with business and interests, or has served in the army, has more experience than his curé, and more real knowledge; his speaking more ungrammatically is of no consequence. But the contrast is still more striking, when this inexperienced priest, who has known nothing but his own seminary, sees at his knees a fashionable, intriguing, impassioned woman, who now, perhaps, at the close of her seventh lustrum, has passed through everything sentimental and ideal. What! *she* ask his advice? *she* call him *father?* Why, every word she utters is a revelation for him—astonishment and fear take possession of his soul. If he is not wise enough to hold his tongue, he will be ridiculous. His penitent, who came to him all trembling, will depart laughing.

IV. There is another difference which will strike only those who are acquainted with the middle ages—*the language was not developed* as it now is. No one being then acquainted with our habits of analysing and developing, confession was naturally reduced to a simple declaration of sin, without any detail of circumstances. Still less could they deduce the phenomena which accompany passion—the desires, doubts, and fears which give it the power of illusion, and make it contagious. There was, if you will, confession; but the woman could not express herself, nor could the priest have understood her; she was not able to reveal the depth of her thought, nor could he have reached it if she had done so. Confession on one side, and sentence on the other, nothing more; there was neither dialogue, confidence, nor disclosing of the heart.

If the priest has not enough imagination and wit to put the questions from the store of his own mind, he has had in his hands for the last two centuries ready-made questions, which he may ask in due order, and by which he will force his fair penitent to dive into her own thoughts, sift her own secrets to deliver them over to him, open her heart's fibres, as one may say, thread by thread, and wind off before him the complete skein, which he henceforth holds in his hands.

This terrible instrument of inquiry, which in unskilful hands may corrupt the soul by its injudicious probing, must necessarily be modified when morals change. Morality does not vary, but morals do, according to the lapse of time; yet this very simple truth never once entered their heads. They have adhered to the morals of the period, when the intellectual movement ceased, as far as they were concerned. The manuals they put into the hands of the young confessor are grounded upon the authority of the casuists, whom Pascal annihilated long ago. Even if the immorality of their solutions had not been demonstrated, remember that Escobar and Sanchez made their questions for a horribly corrupt period, from which, thank God, we are far removed. Their casuistry was from the first addressed to the corrupt and disordered state of society occasioned by long religious warfare. You will find among them crimes that were perhaps never perpetrated, except by the brutal soldiers of the Duke of Alva, or by the exiled, lawless, and godless band that Wallenstein drew after him, a wandering mass of iniquity which would have been abhorred by ancient Sodom.

We know not how to qualify this culpable routine. These books, composed for a barbarous age, unparalleled in crimes, are the same that you give to your pupils in our own civilised age. And this young priest, who, according to your instructions, believes that the world is still that dreadful world, who enters the Confessional with all this villanous science, and his imagination full of monstrous cases, you, imprudent men! (what shall I call you?) you confront him with a child who has never left her mother's side, who knows nothing, has nothing to say, and whose greatest crime is that she has not learned her catechism properly, or has hurt a butterfly!

I shudder at the interrogatories to which he will subject her, and at what he will teach her in his *conscientious brutality*. But he questions her in vain. She knows nothing, and says nothing. He scolds her, and she weeps. Her tears will be soon dried, but it will be long before she ceases to reflect.

A volume might be composed on the first start of the young priest, and his imprudent steps, all fatal either to himself or others. The penitent is occasionally more circumspect than the confessor. She is amused at his proceedings, and looks at him coldly when he becomes animated and goes too far. Sometimes, forgetting himself in his impassioned dream, he is suddenly and roughly awakened by a lesson from an intelligent and satirical woman kneeling before him.

This cruel lesson has given him an icy chill. Confessors do not suffer such a repulse, without remaining a long time bitter, sometimes spiteful for ever. The young priest knew well that he was the victim, the disinherited of this world, but it had not been forced home upon him. Gall drowns his heart. He prays to God (if he can still pray) that the world may perish!

Then returning to his senses, and seeing himself irremediably limed in that black winding-sheet, that death-robe that he will wear to the grave, he shrouds himself within it as he curses it, and muses how he may make the best of his torment.

The only thing he can do, is to strengthen his position as a priest. He has two way of succeeding, either by an understanding with the Jesuits, or by paying a servile court to *Monseigneur* the bishop. I recommend him especially to be violent against the philosophers, and to bark at *pantheism*. Let him also blacken his fellow-priests, and he will appear so much the purer himself. Let him prove himself a thorough hater, and they will forgive him his love.

The Brotherhood will henceforth protect, defend, and cover him. What would have ruined the solitary priest, becomes sanctity itself when he becomes one of a party. Before, he would have been suspended, and sent perhaps for six months to *La Trappe*—now he is made Vicar-general.

Only let him be prudent in the delicate business which the fraternity wishes to conceal; let him learn the arts of priests—to feign, to wait, to know when and how to be satisfied; to advance but slowly, openly, and above ground sometimes, but more often secretly, underneath.

CHAPTER III.

CONFESSION.—THE CONFESSOR AND THE HUSBAND.—HOW THEY DETACH THE WIFE.—THE DIRECTOR.— DIRECTORS ASSOCIATED TOGETHER.—ECCLESIASTICAL POLICY.

When I reflect on all that is contained in the words *confession* and *direction*, those simple words, that immense power, the most complete in the world, and endeavour to analyse their whole meaning, I tremble with fear. I seem to be descending endless spiral stairs into the depths of a dark mine. Just now I felt contempt for the priest; now I fear him.

But we must not be afraid; we must look him in the face. Let us candidly put down in set terms the language of the confessor.

"*God hears you*, hears you through me; through me God will answer you." Such is the first word; such is the literal copy. The authority is accepted as infinite and absolute, without any bargaining as to measure.

"But you tremble, you dare not tell this terrible God your weakness and childishness; well! *tell them to your father*; a father has a right to know the secrets of his child. He is an indulgent father, who wants to know them only to absolve them. He is a sinner like yourself: has he then a right to be severe? Come, then, my child, come and tell me—what you have not dared to whisper in your mother's ear; tell it me; who will ever know?"

Then is it, amid sobs and sighs, from the choking heaving breast that the fatal word rises to the lips: it escapes, and she hides her head. Oh! he who heard that has gained an immense advantage, and will keep it. Would to God that he did not abuse it! It was heard, remember, not by the wood and the dark oak of the confessional, but by ears of flesh and blood.

And this man now knows of this woman, what the husband has not known in all the long effusion of his heart by day and night, what even her own mother does not know, who thinks she knows her entirely, having had her so many times a naked infant upon her knees.

This man knows, and will know—don't be afraid of his forgetting it. If the confession is in good hands, so much the better, for it is for ever. And she, she knows full well she has a master of her intimate thoughts. Never will she pass by that man without casting down her eyes.

The day when this mystery was imparted, he was very near her, she felt it. On a higher seat, he seemed to have an irresistible ascendency over her. A magnetic influence has vanquished her, for she wished not to speak, and she spoke in spite of herself. She felt herself fascinated, like the bird by the serpent.

So far, however, there is no art on the side of the priest. The force of circumstances has done everything, that of religious institution, and that of nature. As a priest, he received her at his knees, and listened to her. Then, master of her secret, of her thoughts, the thoughts of a woman, he became man again, without, perhaps, either wishing or knowing it, and laid upon her, weakened and disarmed, the heavy hand of man.

And her family now? her husband? Who will dare to assert that his position is the same as before?

Every reflecting mind knows full well that thought is the most personal part of the person. The master of a person's thoughts is he to whom the person belongs. The priest has the soul fast, as soon as he has received the dangerous pledge of the first secrets, and he will hold it faster and faster. The two husbands now take shares, for now there are two—one has the soul, the other the body.

Take notice that in this sharing, one of the two really has the whole; the other, if he gets anything, gets it by favour. Thought by its nature is prevailing and absorbing; the master of her thought, in the natural progress of his sway, will ever go on reducing the part that seemed to remain in the possession of the other. The husband may think himself well off, if a widower with respect to the soul, he still preserves the involuntary, inert, and lifeless possession.

How humiliating, to obtain nothing of what was your own, but by authorisation and indulgence;[1] to be seen, and followed into your most private intimacy, by an invisible witness, who governs you and gives you your allowance; to meet in the street a man who knows better than yourself your most secret weaknesses, who bows cringingly, turns and laughs. It is nothing to be powerful, if one is not powerful alone—alone! God does not allow shares.

It is with this reasoning that the priest is sure to comfort himself in his persevering efforts to sever this woman from her family, to weaken her kindred ties, and, particularly, to undermine the rival authority—I mean, the husband's. The husband is a heavy encumbrance to the priest. But if this husband suffers at being so well known, spied, and seen, when he is alone, he who sees all suffers still more. She comes now every moment to tell innocently of things that transport him beyond himself. Often would he stop her, and would willingly say, "Mercy, madam, this is too much!" And though these details make him suffer the torment of the damned, he wants still more, and requires her to enter further and further into these avowals, both humiliating for her, and cruel for him, and to give him the detail of the saddest circumstances.

The Confessor of a young woman may boldly be termed the jealous secret enemy of the husband. If there be one exception to this rule (and I am willing to believe there may be), he is a hero, a saint, a martyr, a man more than man.

The whole business of the confessor is to insulate this woman, and he does it conscientiously. It is the duty of him who leads her in the way of salvation to disengage her gradually from all earthly ties. It requires time, patience, and skill. The question is not how these strong ties may suddenly be broken; but to discover well, first of all, of what threads each tie is composed, and to disentangle, and gnaw them away thread by thread.

And all this may easily be done by him who, awakening new scruples every day, fills a timid soul with uneasiness, about the lawfulness of her most holy affections. If any one of them be innocent, it is, after all, an earthly attachment, a robbery against God: God wants all. No more relationship or friendship; nothing must remain. "A brother?" No, he is still a man. "But at least my sister? my mother?" "No, you must leave all—leave them intentionally, and from your soul; you shall always see them, my child; nothing will appear changed; only, close your heart." A moral solitude is thus established around. Friends go away, offended at her freezing politeness. "People are cool in this house." But why this strange reception? They cannot guess; she does not always know why herself. The thing is commanded; is it not enough? Obedience consists in obeying without reason.

"People are cold here:" this is all that can be said. The husband finds the house larger and more empty. His wife is become quite changed: though present, her mind is absent; she acts as if unconscious of acting; she speaks, but not like herself. Everything is changed in their intimate habits, always for a good reason: "To-day is a fast day"—and to-morrow? "Is a holy-day." The husband respects this austerity; he would consider it very wrong to trouble this exalted devotion; he is sadly resigned: "This becomes embarrassing," says he: "I had not foreseen it; my wife is turning saint."[2]

In this sad house there are fewer friends, yet there is a new one, and a very assiduous one: the habitual confessor is now the director;[3] a great and important change.

As her confessor he received her at church, at regular hours; but as director he visits her at his own hour, sees her at her house, and occasionally at his own.

As confessor he was generally passive, listening much, and speaking little; if he prescribed, it was in a few words; but as director he is all activity; he not only prescribes acts, but what is more important, by intimate conversation he influences her thoughts.

To the confessor she tells her sins; she owes him nothing more; but to the director everything must be told: she must speak of herself and her relations, her business and her interests. When she entrusts to that man her highest interest, that of eternal salvation, how can she help confiding to him her little temporal concerns, the marriage of her children, and the WILL she intends to make? &c., &c.

The confessor is bound to secrecy, he is silent (or ought to be). The director, however, is not so tied down. He may reveal what he knows, especially to a priest, or to another director. Let us suppose about twenty priests assembled in a house (or not quite so many, out of respect for the law against meetings), who may be, some of them the confessors, and others directors of the same persons: as directors they may mutually exchange their information, put upon a table a thousand or two thousand consciences in common, combine their relations, like so many chessmen, regulate beforehand all the movements and interests, and allot to one another the different parts they have to play to bring the whole to their purpose.

The Jesuits alone formerly worked thus in concert; but it is not the fault of the leaders of the clergy, in these days, if the whole of this body, with trembling obedience, do not play at this villanous game. By their all communicating together, their secret revelations might produce a vast mysterious science, which would arm ecclesiastical policy with a power a hundred times stronger than that of the state can possibly be.

Whatever might be wanting in the confession of the master, would easily be supplied by that of his servants and valets. The association of the Blandines of Lyons, imitated in Brittany, Paris, and elsewhere, would alone be sufficient to throw a light upon the whole household of every family. It is in vain they are known, they are nevertheless employed; for they are gentle and docile, serve their masters very well, and know how to see and listen.

Happy the father of a family who has so virtuous a wife, and such gentle, humble, honest, pious servants. What the ancient sighed for, namely, to live in a glass dwelling, where he might be seen by every one, this happy man enjoys without even the expression of a wish. Not a syllable of his is lost. He may speak lower and lower, but a fine ear has caught every word. If he writes down his secret thoughts, not wishing to utter them, they are read:—by whom? No one knows. What he dreams upon his pillow, the next morning, to his great astonishment, he hears in the street.

[1] St. François de Sales, the best of them all, takes compassion on the poor husband. He removes certain scruples of the wife, &c. Even this kindness is singularly humiliating. (See ed. 1833, vol. viii. pp. 254, 312, 347, 348.) Marriage, though one of the sacraments, appears here as a suppliant on its knees before the *direction*, seems to ask pardon, and suffer penance.

[2] For the *insulated state* of a father of a family in Catholic countries, see M. BOUVET'S *Du Catholicisme*, p. 175. (ed. 1840). An English gentleman, whose wife goes to Confession, said to me one day, "I am a lodger in my own house—I come to my meals."—ED.

[3] The name is rare in our days, but the thing is common; he who confesses for a length of time becomes director. Several persons have, at the same time, a confessor, an extraordinary confessor, and a director.

CHAPTER IV.

HABIT.—ITS POWER.—ITS INSENSIBLE BEGINNING.—ITS PROGRESS.—SECOND NATURE.—OFTEN FATAL.—A MAN MAKING THE MOST OF THE POWER OF HABIT.—CAN WE GET CLEAR OF IT?

If spiritual dominion be really of the spirit, if the empire over thought be obtained by thought itself, by a superiority of character and mind, we must give way; we have only to be resigned. Our family may protest, but it will be in vain.

But, for the most part, this is not the case. The influence we speak of by no means supposes, as an essential condition, the brilliant gifts of the mind. They are doubtless of service to him who has them, though, if we have them in a superior degree, they may possibly do him harm. A brilliant superiority, which ever seems a pretension to govern, puts the minds of others on their guard, warns the less prudent, and places an obstacle on the very threshold; which here is everything. People of mediocrity do not alarm us, they gain an entrance more easily. The weaker they are the less they are suspected; therefore are they the stronger in one sense. Iron clashes against the rock, is blunted, and loses its edge and point. But who would distrust water? Weak, colourless, insipid as it is, if, however, it always continues to fall in the same place, it will in time hollow out the flinty rock.

Stand at this window every day, at a certain hour in the afternoon. You will see a pale man pass down the street, with his eyes cast on the ground, and always following the same line of pavement next the houses. Where he set his foot yesterday, there he does to-day, and there he will to-morrow; he would wear out the pavement, if it was never renewed. And by this same street he goes to the same house, ascends to the same story, and in the same cabinet speaks to the same person. He speaks of the same things, and his manner seems the same. The person who listens to him sees no difference between yesterday and to-day:—gentle uniformity, as serene as an infant's sleep, whose breathing raises its chest at equal intervals with the same soft sound.

You think that nothing changes in this monotonous equality; that all these days are the same. You are mistaken; you have *perceived* nothing, yet every day there is a change, slight, it is true, and imperceptible, which the person, himself changed by little and little, does not remark.

It is like a dream in a bark. What distance have you come, whilst you were dreaming? Who can tell? Thus you go on, without seeming to move— still, and yet rapidly. Once out of the river, or canal, you soon find yourself at sea; the uniform immensity in which you now are will inform you still less of the distance you go. Time and place are equally uncertain; no sure point to occupy attention; and attention itself is gone. The reverie is profound, and becomes more and more so:—an ocean of dreams upon the smooth ocean of waters.

A pleasant state, in which everything becomes insensible, even gentleness itself. Is it death, or is it life? To distinguish, we require attention, and we should awake from our dream.—No, let it go on, whatever it may be that carries me along with it, whether it lead me to life or death.

Alas! 'tis habit! that gently sloping formidable abyss, into which we slide so easily! we may say everything that is bad of it, and, also, everything that is good, and it will be always true.

Let us be frank: if the action that we did in the first instance knowingly and voluntarily, was never done but with will and attention, if it never became habitual and easy, we should act but little and slowly, and our life would pass away in endeavours and efforts. If, for instance, every time we stepped forward we had to reflect upon our direction, and how to keep our balance, we should not walk much better than the child who is trying to go alone. But walking soon becomes a habit, an action that is performed without any need of invoking the constant and intermediate operation of the will. It is the same with many other acts which, still less voluntary, become at last mechanical, automatical, foreign, as I may say, to our personality. As we advance in life a considerable portion of our activity escapes our notice, removes from the sphere of liberty to enter that of habit, and becomes as it were fated; the remainder, relieved in that respect, and so far absolved from attention and effort, finds itself, by a process of compensation, more free to act elsewhere.

This is useful, but it is also dangerous. The fatal part increases within us, without our interference, and grows in the darkness of our inward nature. What formerly struck our attention, now passes unperceived. What was at first difficult, in time grows easy, too easy: at last we can no longer say even that it is easy, for it takes place of its own accord, independently of our will; we suffer, if we do not do it. These acts being those, of all others, that cost the least trouble, are incessantly renewed. We must, at last, confess that a second nature is the result, which, formed at the expense of the former, becomes, in a great measure, its substitute. We forget the difficulties of our early beginnings, and fancy we have always been so. This favours at least our idleness, and excuses us from making any efforts to stop ourselves on the brink. Besides, the very traces of the change are at length effaced, the road has disappeared; even though we desire to go back, we could not. It is as though a bridge were broken down behind us; we have passed over it—but for the last time.

We then resign ourselves to our lot, and say, with a faint attempt to smile, "*For me it is a second nature*," or, better still, "*It is my nature*." So much have we forgotten! But between this nature and our real primitive nature, which we received at our birth, there is a great difference; which is, that the latter, derived from the bosom of the mother, was like the real mother herself, an attentive guardian of life, that warned us of whatever may compromise it, that sought and found in its benevolence a remedy for our ills. Whereas this second nature, habit, under this perfidious name is often nothing else than the high road that leads to death.

"It is my second nature," says the opium drinker in a sad tone, when he sees dying by his side one who had taken to the deadly beverage only a few months before himself: "I have still so many months to live." "It is my second nature," says a miserable child, a devoted victim of idle and bad habits. Neither reasoning, chastisement, nor maternal grief, is of any avail. They both go, and will go, to the end, following the road by which people travel but once.

A vulgar proverb (but too true in this case) tells us, "*Whoever has once drunk, will drink*." We must generalise it, and say, "*Whoever has acted, will act; whoever has suffered, will suffer*." But this is still more true with respect to passive than active habits. Accustomed to let things take their course, to suffer and to enjoy, we become incapable of resuming our activity. At last we do not even require the enticement of pleasure; even when it is no more, and pain usurps its place, inexorable habit pours out still from the same cup: it then no longer takes the trouble to dissemble; we recognise, when too late, how ugly and invincible this tyrant is, who says coldly, "You drank the honey first, now you shall drink the gall, and to the last drop."

If this tyrant, habit, is so strong when it acts blindly, when it is only a thing such as opium or gin, what does it become when it has eyes, a will, *an art*, in a word, when it is a man? A man full of calculation, who knows how to create and cherish habit for his own advantage, a man who for his first means brings against you your belief; who begins personal fascination in the authority of a respected character; who, to exercise it over you and create a habit in you, has daily occasions, days, months, years, time, irresistible time, the tamer of all human things, time, that can eat away iron and brass! Is the heart of woman hard enough to resist it?

A woman? a child! still less, a person *who will be a child*, who employs all the faculties she has acquired since childhood to fall back into childishness, who directs her will to wish no longer, and her thoughts no longer to know anything, and gives herself up as if asleep.

Suppose her to awake (it is a very rare case), to awake for a moment (surprising the tyrant without his mask, seeing him as he really is), and then to wish to escape. Do you think she can? To do so, she must act; but she no longer knows what it is, not having acted for so long a time; her limbs are stiff; her legs are paralysed and have lost all motion; her heavy hand rises, falls again, and refuses.

Then you may perceive too well what is habit, and how, once bound in its thousand imperceptible threads, you remain tied in spite of you to what you detest. These threads, though they escape the eye, are, nevertheless, tough. Pliable and supple as they seem to be, you may break through one, but underneath you find two; it is a double, nay triple, net. Who can know its thickness?

I read once in an old story what is really touching, and very significant. It was about a woman, a wandering princess, who, after many sufferings, found for her asylum a deserted palace, in the midst of a forest. She felt happy in reposing there, and remaining some time: she went to and fro from one large empty room to another, without meeting with any obstacle; she thought herself alone and free. All the doors were open. Only at the hall-door, no one having passed through since herself, the spider had woven his web in the sun, a thin, light, and almost invisible network; a feeble obstacle which the princess, who wishes at last to go out, thinks she can remove without any difficulty. She raises the web; but there is another behind it, which she also raises without trouble. The second concealed a third, that she must also raise:—strange! there are four.—No, five! or rather six—and more beyond. Alas! how will she get rid of so many? She is already tired. No matter! she perseveres; by taking breath a little she may continue. But the web continues too, and is ever renewed with a malicious obstinacy. What is she to do? She is overcome with fatigue and perspiration, her arms fall by her sides. At last, exhausted as she is, she sits down on the ground, on that insurmountable threshold:—she looks mournfully at the aerial obstacle fluttering in the wind, lightly and triumphantly.—Poor princess! poor fly! now you are caught! But why did you stay in that fairy dwelling, and give the spider time to spin his web?

CHAPTER V.

ON CONVENTS—OMNIPOTENCE OF THE DIRECTOR.—
CONDITION OF THE NUN FORLORN AND WATCHED.—
CONVENTS THAT ARE AT THE SAME TIME BRIDEWELLS
AND BEDLAMS.—INVEIGLING.—BARBAROUS
DISCIPLINE.—STRUGGLE BETWEEN THE SUPERIOR NUN
AND THE DIRECTOR.—CHANGE OF DIRECTORS.—THE
MAGISTRATE.

Fifteen years ago I occupied, in a very solitary part of the town, a house, the garden of which was adjacent to that of a convent of women. Though my windows overlooked the greatest part of their garden, I had never seen my sad neighbours. In the month of May, on Rogation-day, I heard numerous weak, very weak voices, chanting prayers, as the procession passed through the convent garden. The singing was sad, dry, unpleasant, their voices false, as if spoiled by sufferings. I thought for a moment they were chanting prayers for the dead; but, listening more attentively, I distinguished on the contrary, "*Te rogamus, audi nos,*" the song of hope which invokes the benediction of the God of life upon fruitful nature. This May-song, chanted by these lifeless nuns, offered to me a bitter contrast. To see these pale girls crawling along on the flowery, verdant turf, these poor girls; who will never bloom again!—The thought of the middle ages that had at first flashed across my mind soon died away: for then monastic life was connected with a thousand other things; but in our modern harmony what is this but a barbarous contradiction, a false, harsh, grating note? What I then beheld before me was to be defended neither by nature nor by history. I shut my window again, and sadly resumed my book. This sight had been painful to me, as it was not softened or atoned for by any poetical sentiment. It reminded me much less of chastity than of sterile widowhood, a state of emptiness, inaction, disgust—of an intellectual[1] and moral fast, the state in which these unfortunate creatures are kept by their absolute rulers.

We were speaking of habit; it is certainly there that it reigns a tyrant. Very little art is required to rule over these poor, insulated, immured, and dependent women; as there is no outward influence to counterbalance the impression that one person, ever the same person, makes on them daily. The least skilful priest may easily fascinate their natures, already weakened, and brought down to the most servile, trembling obedience. There is little courage or merit in thus trampling over the creature which is already crushed.

To speak first of the power of habit: nothing of all that we see in the world can give us an idea of the force with which it acts upon this little immured community. Family society, doubtless, modifies us, but its influence is neutralised by outward events. The regularity with which our favourite newspaper comes every morning with uniform monotony, has certainly some influence; but this newspaper has its rivals, its opponents. Another influence which exists less in our time, but is still very powerful over secluded persons, is that of a book, the captivating perusal of which may detain us for months and years. Diderot confesses that Clarissa was read by him over and over again, and that it was for a long time his very life, his joy, his grief, his summer and winter. But the finest thing of this class is, after all, but a book, a dumb, inanimate thing, which, though you may call it as animate as you please, does not hear, and cannot answer; it has no words with which it may answer yours, nor eyes to reflect your own.

Away, then, with books, those cold paper images!

Imagine in a monastery, where nothing else intrudes, the only living object, the only person who has a right to enter, who monopolises all the influences of which we have spoken, who is, in himself, their society, newspaper, novel, and sermon; a person whose visit is the only interruption to the deadly monotony of a life devoid of employment. Before he comes, and after he has been, is the only division of time in this life of profound monotony.

We said a person, we ought to have said a man. Whoever will be candid would confess that a woman would never have this influence; that the circumstance of his being of the opposite sex has much to do with it, even with the purest and with those who had never dreamed of sex.

To be the only one, without either comparison or contradiction, to be the whole world of a soul, to wean it, at pleasure, from every reminiscence that might cause any rivalry, and efface from this docile heart even the thought of a mother that might still[2] be cherished within it! To inherit everything, and remain alone and be master of this heart by the extinction of all natural sentiments!

The only one! But this is the good, the perfect, the amiable, the beloved! Enumerate every good quality, and they will all be found to be contained in this one term. A thing even (not to say a person), a thing, if it be the only one, will in time captivate our hearts. Charlemagne, seeing from his palace always the same sight, a lake with its verdant border, at last fell in love with it.

Habit certainly contributes much; but also that great necessity of the heart to tell everything to what we are always in the habit of seeing: whether it be man or thing, we must speak. Even if it were a stone, we should tell it everything, for our thoughts must be told, and our griefs be poured out from an overflowing heart.

Do you believe that this poor nun is tranquil in this life so monotonous? How many sad, but, alas! too true confessions I could relate here, that have been communicated to me by tender female friends, who had gone and received their tears in their bosom, and returned, pierced to the heart, to weep with me.

What we must wish for the prisoner is, that her heart, and almost her body, may die. If she be not shattered and crushed into a state of self-oblivion, she will find in the convent the united sufferings of solitude and of the world. Alone, without being able to be alone![3] Forlorn, yet all her actions watched!

Forlorn! This nun still young, yet already old through abstinence and grief, was yesterday a boarder, a novice whom they caressed. The friendship of the young girls, the maternal flattery of the old, her attachment for this nun, or that confessor, everything deceived her, and enticed her onward to eternal confinement. We almost always fancy ourselves called to God, when we follow an amiable, enchanting person, one who, with that smiling, captivating devotion, delights in this sort of spiritual conquest. As soon as one is gained, she goes to another; but the poor girl who followed her, in the belief that she was loved, is no longer cared for.

Alone, in a solitude without tranquillity of mind, and without repose. How sweet, in comparison with this, would be the solitude of the woods! The trees would still have compassion; they are not so insensible as they seem: they hear and they listen.

A woman's heart, that unconquerable maternal instinct, the basis of a woman's character, tries to deceive itself. She will soon find out some young friend, some candid companion, a favourite pupil. Alas! she will be taken from her. The jealous ones, to find favour with the superiors, never fail to accuse the purest attachments. The devil is jealous, in the interest of God—he makes his objections for the sake of God alone.

What wonder, then, if this woman is sad, sadder every day, frequenting the most melancholy-looking avenues, and no longer speaks? Then her solitude becomes a crime. Now she is pointed out as suspected: they all observe and watch her. In the day-time? It is not enough. The spy system lasts all night: they watch her sleeping, listen to her when she dreams, and take down her words.

The dreadful feeling of being thus watched night and day must strangely trouble all the powers of the soul. The darkest hallucinations come over her, and all those wicked dreams that her poor reason, when on the point of leaving her, can make in broad daylight and wide awake. You know the visions that Piranesi has engraved: vast subterraneous prisons, deep pits without air, staircases that you ascend for ever without reaching the top, bridges that lead to an abyss, low vaults, narrow passages of catacombs growing closer and closer. In these dreadful prisons, which are punishments, you may perceive, moreover, instruments of torture, wheels, iron collars, whips.

In what, I should like to know, do convents of our time differ from houses of correction and mad-houses?[4] Many convents seem to unite the three characters.

I know but one difference between them; whilst the houses of correction are inspected by the law, and the mad-houses by the police, both stop at the convent doors; the law is afraid, and dares not pass the threshold.

The inspection of convents, and the precise designation of their character, are, however, so much more indispensable in these days, as they differ in a very serious point from the convents of the old *régime*.

Those of the last century were properly asylums, where, for a donation once paid, every noble family, whether living as nobles, or rich citizens, placed one or more daughters to make a rich son. Once shut up there, they might live or die as they pleased; they were no longer cared for. But now *nuns inherit*, they become an object to be gained, a prey for a hundred thousand snares—an easy prey in their state of captivity and dependence. A superior, zealous to enrich her community, has infallible means to force the nun to give up her wealth; she can a hundred times a-day, under pretence of devotion and penitence, humble, vex, and even ill-treat her, till she reduces her to despair. Who can say where asceticism finishes and captation begins, that "*compelle intrare*" applied to fortune? A financial and administrative spirit prevails to such a degree in our convents, that this sort of talent is what they require in a superior before every other. Many of these ladies are excellent managers. One of them is known in Paris by the notaries and lawyers, as able to give them lessons in matters of donations, successions, and wills. Paris need no longer envy Bologna that learned female jurisconsult, who, occasionally wrapped in a veil, professed in the chair of her father.

Our modern laws, which date from the Revolution, and which, in their equity, have determined that the daughter and younger son should not be without their inheritance, work powerfully in this respect in favour of the counter-revolution: and that explains the rapid and unheard-of increase of religious houses.

Nothing stops the monastic recruiters in their zeal for the salvation of rich souls. You may see them fluttering about heirs and heiresses. What a premium for the young peasants who people our seminaries is this prospect of power! Once priests, they may direct fortunes as well as consciences![5]

Captation, so conspicuous in the busy world, is not so in the convents; though it is here still more dangerous, being exercised over persons immured and dependent. There it reigns unbridled, and is formidable with impunity. For who can know it? Who dares enter here? No one. Strange! There are houses in France that are estranged to France. The street is still France; but pass yonder threshold, and you are in a foreign country which laughs at your laws.

What, then, are their laws? We are ignorant upon the subject. But we know for certain (for no pains are taken to disguise it) that the barbarous discipline of the middle ages is preserved in full force. Cruel contradiction! This system that speaks so much of the distinction of the soul and the body, and believes it, since it boldly exposes the confessor to carnal temptations! Well! this very same system teaches us that the body, distinct from the soul, modifies it by its suffering; that the soul improves and becomes more pure under the lash![6] It preaches spiritualism to meet valiantly the seduction of the flesh, and materialism when required to annihilate the will!

What! when the law forbids to strike even our galley slaves, who are thieves, murderers, the most ferocious of men—you men of grace, who speak only of charity, *the good holy Virgin, and the gentle Jesus*—you strike women!—nay, girls, even children—who, after all, are only guilty of some trifling weakness!

How are these chastisements administered? This is a question, perhaps, still more serious. What sort of terms of composition may not be extorted by fear? At what price does authority sell its indulgence?

Who regulates the number of stripes? Is it you, My Lady Abbess? or you, Father Superior? What must be the capricious partial decision of one woman against another, if the latter displeases her; an ugly woman against a handsome one, or an old one against a young girl? We shudder to think.

A strange struggle often happens between the superior nun and the director. The latter, however hardened he may be, is still a man. It is very difficult for him at last not to be affected for the poor girl, who tells him everything, and obeys him implicitly. Female authority perceives it instantly, observes him, and follows him closely. He sees his penitent but little, very little, but it is always thought too much. The confession shall last only so many minutes: they wait for him, watch in hand. It would last too long, nay, for ever, without this precaution. To the poor recluse, who received from every one else only insult and ill-treatment, a compassionate confessor is still a welcome refuge.

We have known superiors demand and obtain several times from their bishops a change of confessors, without finding any sufficiently austere. There is ever a wide difference between the harshness of man and the cruelty of a woman! What is, in your opinion, the most faithful incarnation of the devil in this world? Some inquisitor? Some Jesuit or other? No, a *female Jesuit*,—some great lady, who has been converted, and believes herself born to rule, who among this flock of trembling females acts the Bonaparte, and who, more absolute than the most absolute tyrant, uses the rage of her badly-cured passions to torment her unfortunate defenceless sisters.

Far from being the adversary of the confessor in this case, he has my best wishes. Whether he be priest, monk, or Jesuit, I am now on his side. I entreat him to interfere, if he can. In this hell, where the law cannot penetrate, he is the only person who can say a word of humanity. I know very well that this interference will create the strongest and most dangerous attachment. The heart of the poor young creature is wholly given up beforehand to him who defends her.

The priest will be removed, driven away, and ruined, if it be necessary. Nothing is easier to an active influential superior. He dares not venture there, is afraid of disturbance, and retires timidly. You will find neither priests nor prelates in these cases mindful of their power, as confessors and spiritual judges; nor will they refuse absolution to the tyrant of the nuns, as Las Casas did to those of the Indians.

There are, fortunately, other judges. The law sleeps, but it still lives.[7] Some courageous magistrates have been willing to do their duty.[8] No doubt they will be permitted. The nights of the guilty have been troubled; they know that every violence which is committed there, every blow given in defiance of the law, is an accusation against them before heaven and earth. *Exsurge, Domine, et judica causam tuam!*

[1] I have already spoken of Sister Mary Lemonnier, persecuted for knowing too well how to write and draw flowers, &c.—"My confessor," says she, "forbade me to gather

flowers and to draw. Unfortunately, walking in the garden with the nuns, there were on the edge of the grass two wild poppies, which, without any intention, I lopped between my fingers in passing. One of the sisters saw me, and ran to inform the superior nun who was walking in front, and who immediately came towards me, made me open my hand, and, seeing the poppies, told me that I had done for myself. And the confessor having come the same evening, she accused me before him of disobedience in having gathered flowers. It was in vain I told him that it was unintentionally done, and that they were only wild poppies; I could not obtain permission to confess myself."—*Note of Sister Marie Lemonnier*, in Mr. Tilliard's Mémoire. The newspapers and the reviews in March, 1845, give extracts from it.

[2] It is often from an instinctive tyranny that the superiors delight in breaking the ties of kindred. "The curate of my parish exhorted me to write to my father, who had just lost my mother. I let Advent go by (during which time nuns are not permitted to write letters), and the latter days of the month which are passed in retirement in the institution to prepare us for the renewing of our vows, which takes place on new-year's day. But after the holy term I hastened to fulfil my duty towards the best of fathers by addressing to him both my prayers and good wishes, and endeavouring to offer him some consolation in the afflictions and trials with which it had pleased God to visit him. I went to the cell of the superior nun to beg her to read over my letter, fix the convent seal to it, and send it off; but she was not there. I therefore put it in my cell upon the table, and went to prayers; during which time our reverend mother the superior, who knew that I had written, because she had sent one of the nuns to see what I was about, beckoned to one of the sisters and bid her go and take my

letter. She did so every time I wrote, seven times running, so that my father died five months afterwards without ever obtaining a letter from me, which he had so much desired, and had even asked me for on his death-bed, by the curate of his parish."—*Note of Sister Lemonnier* in Mr. Tilliard's Mémoire. See also the *National*, March, 1845.

[3] The preliminary confession of the nuns to the superior, easily acceded to in the first fit of enthusiasm, soon becomes an intolerable vexation. Even in Madame de Chantal's time, it was much complained of. See her letters, and Fichet, 256; also Ribadeneira, Life of St. Theresa.

[4] Sister Marie Lemonnier was shut up with mad girls: here she found a Carmelite nun, who had been there nine years. The third volume of the *Wandering Jew* contains the real history of Mademoiselle B. All this happened very lately, not in a mad-house, but in a convent. Since I have this opportunity of saying a word to our admirable novelist, let him permit me to ask him why he thought proper to idealise the Jesuits to this extent? who does not know that certain dignitaries of their order have become immortal by ridicule? It is difficult to believe stupid writers to be strong minds, or profound machinators. I look in vain for a Rodin, and find only Loriquets.

[5] All these people buy and sell, and become brokers. Prelates speculate in lands and buildings, the Lazarists turn agents for military recruits, &c. The latter, the successors of St. Vincent de Paul, the directors of our Sisters of Charity, have been so blessed by God for their charity, that they have now a capital of twenty millions. Their present chief, Mr. Etienne, then a procurer of the order, was lately the Lazarist agent in a distillery company. The very important law-suit they have at the present moment will decide whether a society engaged

by a general, its absolute chief, is freed from every engagement by a change of generals.

[6] Did not this horrible art calculate well on the influence of the body? this art that does not awaken man's energy by pain, but enervates it by diet and the misery of dungeons! (See Mabillon's Treatise on Monastic Prisons.) The revelations of the prisoners of Spielberg have enlightened us upon this head.

[7] The affairs at Avignon, Sens, Poictiers, though the guilty parties have been but slightly punished, permit us to hope that the law will at length awake. We read in one of the newspapers of Caen: "A report was current yesterday at the *palais*, that the *procureur-général* was going to evoke not only the affair of the sequestration of Sister Marie, but also that of Sister Ste-Placide, about whose removal the *avocat-général*, Sorbier, wrote to the under-prefect of Bayeux, on the 13th of August last. Lastly, that of Madmlle. H——, of Rouen, whom the attorney-general (*procureur du roi*), of Rouen, was obliged to remove from the establishment of Bon-Sauveur."—*National* (newspaper), March 10, 1845.

[8] The inspection of convents ought to be shared between the judiciary and municipal magistracy, and the administrations of charity. The bar is too much occupied to be able to undertake it alone. If these houses are necessary as asylums for poor women, who earn too little in a solitary life, at least let them be free asylums like the *béguinages* of Flanders; but not under the same direction. When a woman has ended the task of the wife, she begins that of the mother or grandmother.

CHAPTER VI.

ABSORPTION OF THE WILL.—GOVERNMENT OF ACTS, THOUGHTS, AND WILLS.—ASSIMILATION.—TRANSHUMANATION.—TO BECOME THE GOD OF ANOTHER.—PRIDE.—PRIDE AND DESIRE.

If we believe politicians, happiness consists in reigning. They sincerely think so, since they accept in exchange for happiness so much trouble and so many annoyances; a martyrdom often that perhaps the saints would have shrunk from.

But the reign must be real. Are we quite sure that it is really to reign, to make ordinances that are not executed, to enact with great effort, and as a supreme victory, one law more, which is doomed to sleep in the bulletin of laws at the side of thirty thousand of the same kin?

It is of no use to prescribe acts, if we are not first masters of the mind; in order to govern the bodily world, we must reign in the intellectual world. This is the opinion of the thinking man, the profound writer; and he believes he reigns. He is, indeed, a king; at least for the next age. If he is really original, he outsteps his century, and is postponed till another time. But he will reign to-morrow, and the day after, and so on for ages, and ever more absolute. To-day he will be alone; every success costs a friend, but he acquires others; and I am willing to believe both ardent and numerous; those he loses were, no doubt, worth less, but they were those he loved; and he will never see the others. Work, then, disinterested man, work on; you will have for your reward a little noise and smoke. Is not that a sufficient reward for you? King of ages yet unborn, you will live and die empty-handed. On the shore of that sea of unknown ages, you, a child, have picked up a shell, which you hold to your ear, to try to catch a faint sound, in which you fancy you hear your own name.

Look on the other hand at that man, that *Priest*, who at the very time he is telling us his kingdom is above, has adroitly secured for himself the reality of the earth beneath. He lets you go, as you please, in search of unknown worlds; but he himself seizes on the present one; your own world, poor dreamer! that which you loved, the nest where you hoped to come back and be cherished. Accuse no one but yourself, it is your own fault. With your eyes turned towards the dawn you forgot yourself, whilst you were peeping to catch a glimpse of the first ray of the future. You turn round when it is rather too late; another possesses the cherished casket in which you had left your heart.

The sovereignty of ideas is not that of the will. We can only get possession of the will by the will itself: not general and vague, but an especial and personal will, which attaches itself perseveringly to, and really commands, the person, because it makes it in its own image.

Really to reign, is to reign over a soul. What are all the thrones in comparison to this kingly sway? What is dominion over an unknown crowd? The really ambitious have been too shrewd to make a mistake! They have not exhausted their efforts in the extension of a vague and weak power, which loses by being extended; they have aimed rather at its solidity, intensity, and immutable possession.

The end thus settled, the priest has a great advantage which no one else possesses. His business is with a soul *which gives itself up of its own accord.* The great obstacle for other powers is, that they do not well know the person acted upon; they see only the outside, but the priest looks within.

Whether he be clever, or only of an ordinary stamp, still, by the sole virtue of hopes and fears, by that magic key which opens the world to come, the priest opens also the heart, and that heart wishes to lay itself open; all its fear is lest it should conceal anything. It does not see itself entirely; but whenever it is at a loss, the priest sees his way clearly, and penetrates into it, by the simple method of obtaining revelations from servants, friends, and relatives, and comparing them together. With all this enlightening he forms a mass of light, which, concentrated upon the object, renders it so thoroughly luminous, that he knows not only its present existence, but its future state, deciphering, from the very first day, in its instinct and sentiment, what will be its thoughts on the morrow. He, therefore, truly knows this heart, both by sight and foresight. This rare science would remain inexplicable without a word in explanation. If it knows its subject to this degree, it is because it is its own work. The director creates the directed; the latter is his work, and becomes in time one and the same man. How is it possible the former should not know the ideas and wishes which he himself has inspired, and which are his own? A transfusion takes place between the two in this incessant action, in which the inferior, receiving everything from the other, goes on gradually losing his personality. Growing weaker and more idle every day, he thinks himself happy in no longer having a will of his own, and is glad to see that troublesome will, which has caused too many sufferings, die away and be lost. Even so a wounded man sees his blood, his life-blood flowing away, and feels himself the easier.

But who is to make good within you, and fill up the void left by this draining away of moral personality, by which you escape from yourself?— In two letters—*he*.

He, the patient, cunning man, who, day by day, taking from you a little of yourself, and substituting a little of himself, has gently subtilised the one, and put the other in its place. The soft and weak nature of women, almost as yielding as that of children, is well adapted for this transfusion. The same woman seeing ever the same man, takes without knowing it, his turn of mind, his accent, his language, nay more, something of his gait and physiognomy. She speaks as he does, and walks in the same manner as he. In only seeing her pass by, a person of any penetration would see that *she is he*.

But this outward similarity is but a weak sign of the profound change within. What has been transformed is the intimate, most intimate part. A great mystery has been effected, that which Dante calls *transhumanation*; when a human person, melting away without knowing it, has assumed (substance for substance) another humanity; when the superior replacing the inferior, the agent the patient, no longer needs to direct him, but becomes his being. *He* is, the other is not; unless we consider him as an accident, a quality of this being, a pure phenomenon, an empty shadow, a nothing.

Why did we just now speak of influence, dominion, and royalty? This is a much higher thing than royalty—this is divinity. It is to be the god of another.

If there be in this world an occasion on which we may become mad, it is this. The thought of the man who has reached this point, in whatever humility he may cloak himself, is that of the pagan: "Deus factus sum!" I was a man, I am God!

More than God. He will say to his creature, "God had created you so, and I have made you another person; so that being no longer His, but mine, you are myself, my inferior self, who are only to be distinguished from myself by your adoring me."

Dependent creature, how could you have helped yielding?—God yields to my word when I make Him descend to the altar. Christ becomes humble and docile, and comes down at my hour, at my sign, to take the place of the bread that is no more.[1]

We are no longer surprised at the furious pride of the priest, who, in his royalty of Rome, has often carried it to greater extremes than all the follies of the emperors, making him despise not only men and things, but his own oath, and the word which he gave as infallible. Every priest being able to make God, can just as well make odd even, or things done things undone, things said things unsaid. The angel is afraid of so much power, and stands back respectfully before this man to see him pass.[2]

Go, boast to me now of your privations and mortifications! I am indeed much touched by them!—Do you think, then, that through that plain robe and meagre body, ay, in that pale heart I do not see the deep, exquisite and maddening enjoyment of pride, which composes the very being of a priest? What he carries within his robe, and broods over so jealously, is a treasure of terrific pride. His hands tremble with it: a bright ray of delight gleams in his downcast eyes.

Oh! with what fervour he hates everything that is an obstacle to him, everything that prevents his infinity from being indeed infinite! How does he desire with all his infinite heart to annihilate it! Oh! how diabolical it is to hate in God!

A great suffering is connected with this great enjoyment of being the god of another soul: all that is wanting to complete this divinity causes horrible pangs. You cannot be surprised if this man pursues with an insatiable ardour the absorption of a soul which he hopes to assimilate. You may easily understand the real and profound cause of this strange avidity, which wants to see and know everything, both the trivial and the important, the principal and the accessory, the essential and the indifferent, and which, not satisfied with enveloping it outwardly, tries to reach the bottom, and probing lower and lower in the very depth, would attain the essence. Suppose even this to be reached, still it will cry out for—more! Alas! it may ever acquire more, and again more; but something will ever remain beyond. Who can measure a soul? It preserves in its recesses, unknown to itself (and to you also), both space and depth. That soul which seemed to you already acquired, and which you thought in your entire possession, hides behind it, perhaps, a world of liberty which you can never reach.

This is humiliating, gloomy, nay, almost despair. Horrible suffering! not to have all, is, for a god, to have nothing.

Then, even then, in their very pride, an ironical voice is heard, scoffing at their pride; it is the voice of desire, which it had silenced till now: "Poor god," says she, "you are no god; it is your own fault; I told you so before. Come, leave off your school-divinity, and your *distinguo* of the corporeal and spiritual natures. To possess, is to have all. He alone has possession who can both use and abuse. For the soul to be really thine, one thing is still wanting—the body."

[1] "Origen thinks that the priest must be a little God, to do an act that is beyond the power of angels." Father Fichet (a Jesuit), "Life of Madame de Chantal." p. 615. If you require a more serious Jesuit than Fichet, here is Bourdaloue: "Though the priest be in this sacrifice only the substitute of Jesus Christ, it is nevertheless certain, that Jesus Christ *submits to him*, that He *becomes his subject*, and renders him, every day upon our altars, *the most prompt and exact obedience*. If faith did not teach us these truths, could we think that a man could ever attain to such an elevation, and be invested with a character that enables him, if I may say so, to *command* his sovereign Lord, and make Him descend from heaven?"

[2] One of the new priests, under the orders of St. François de Sales often saw his guardian angel. Having arrived at the church-door, he stopped. They asked him the reason: he answered ingenuously, that "he was accustomed to see his guardian angel walk before him, and that this prince of heaven *had then stopped and stood aside, out of respect for his character, giving him the precedence.*"—Maupas du Tour, Life of St. François de Sales, p. 199.

CHAPTER VII.

DESIRE.—ABSORPTION AND ASSIMILATION CONTINUED.—
TERRORS OF THE OTHER WORLD.—THE PHYSICIAN AND
THE PATIENT.—ALTERNATIVES.—POSTPONEMENTS.—
THE EFFECTS OF FEAR IN LOVE.—TO BE ALL-POWERFUL
AND ABSTAIN.—STRUGGLES BETWEEN THE SPIRIT AND
THE FLESH.—MORAL DEATH MORE POTENT THAN
PHYSICAL LIFE.—IT CANNOT REVIVE.

Let us a pause a moment at the brink of the abyss that we have just
had a glimpse of, and before we descend into it, let us know well where we
are.

The unlimited dominion, of which we spoke just now, could never be
sufficiently explained by the power of habit, strengthened by all the arts of
seduction and captation; it would be especially impossible to understand
how so many inferior men succeed in obtaining their ends. We must repeat
here what we have said elsewhere: *If this power of death has so much hold upon the
soul, the reason is, that it generally attacks it in its dying state*; when weakened by
worldly passions, and crushing it more and more by the ebb and flow of
religious passions, it finds at last that it has neither strength, nor nerve, nor
anything that can offer resistance.

Which of us has not known, in his life, those moments when violent
activity having ruffled our hearts, we hate action, liberty, and ourselves?—
when the wave that bore us upon its gentle but treacherous bosom retires
suddenly and harshly from beneath, leaving us upon the dry strand—where
we remain like a log? Never could the soul, thus stranded, be set in motion
again, if it were not, independently of its will, floated off by the waves of
Lethe. A low voice then says, "Move not; act no more, do not even wish;
die in will."—"Happy release! wish for me! There, I give up to you that
troublesome liberty, the weight of which oppressed me so much. A soft
pillow of faith, a childish obedience is all I now want. Now I shall sleep
happily!"

But such people do not sleep, they only dream. How can they,
nervous and trembling with weakness, expect to repose? They lie still, it is
true; but they are also plunged in dreams. The soul will not act, but the
imagination acts without her; and this involuntary fluctuation is but the
more fatiguing. Then, all the terrors of childhood crowd upon the patient,

and more steadfastly than they did upon the child. The phantasmagoria of the middle ages, which we thought forgotten, revives; the dark infernal region of hell, which we had laughed away, exacts a heavy interest, and takes a cruel revenge: this poor soul belongs to it. What would become of her, alas! had she not a spiritual physician at her bedside to succour and encourage her? "Do not leave me, I am too much afraid!"—"Do not fear; you are not responsible for all this: God will pardon you these disordered emotions; they are not yours; the devil stirs thus within us."—"The devil! ah! I felt him; I thought, indeed, this violent and strange emotion was foreign to me. But how horrible to be the sport of the malignant spirit!"— "I am here; be not afraid; hold me fast; go straight on; the abyss, it is true, is gaping wide, on the right and on the left; but, by following the narrow bridge, with God's assistance, we shall walk along this razor-edge to Paradise."

Great, indeed, is the power to be so necessary, ever called and desired! to hold, as it were, the two threads of hope and fear, which drag the soul at pleasure. When troubled, they calm her; when calm, they agitate her: she grows more and more feeble, and the physician is so much the stronger; he perceives it, and he enjoys it. He, to whom every natural enjoyment is forbidden, feels a gloomy happiness, a mawkish sensuality, in exercising this power; making the ebb and the flow, afflicting in order to console, wounding, healing, and wounding again. "Oh! let her be ill for ever! I suffer, let her suffer with me. It is at least something to have pain in common."

But they do not gather these sighs, and support the languid head with impunity. He who wounded, is wounded in his turn. In these outpourings of the heart, the most simple person often says, without knowing it, things that inflame the passions. He draws back, as if indignant and angry, before the scorching flame that a gentle hand has applied without being aware of it: he endeavours to conceal his emotion under a well-feigned pious anger; he tries to hate sin, but he only envies it.

How gloomy he seems that day! See him ascend the pulpit. What ails this holy man of God? People see too plainly; it is the zeal of the law that devours him—he bears all the sins of the people. What thunder and lightning in his discourse! is it the last judgment? every one flinches. One woman, however, has received the whole force of the thundering denunciation; she grows pale, her knees no longer support her; the blow struck home: for he who knows her inmost soul found too easily the terrible word, the only word that could strike and touch her to the quick. She alone felt it; she finds herself now alone in the church (the crowd no longer exists for her), and alone she sees herself falling into the infernal dark abyss. "Father, reach me your hand! I feel I am sinking!"

Not yet, it is not yet time! She must struggle and fall still lower, then rise a little to sink lower still. Now, she comes to him every day more grieving, and more pressing. How she prays and insists! But she will not yet get the comforting word: "To-day? No, on Saturday." And on Saturday he puts her off till Wednesday.[1] What! three days and three whole nights in the same anxiety? She weeps like a child. No matter; he resists and leaves her, but he is troubled even in resisting her. In thus humbling this *belle madame*, he tastes a secret pleasure of pride; and yet he thinks himself that he has been too harsh towards her: he loves her, and he has made her weep!

Cruel man! do you not see that the poor woman is dying? that she is becoming weaker at every burst of grief? What is it you want? her downfall? But in this prostration of strength, in this terror of despair and abandonment of dignity, is there not already a complete downfall? No; what he wants till now, is, that she may suffer as he does, resemble him in sufferings, and be his partner in his woes and frenzy. He is alone; then let her be alone. He has no family; he hates her as a wife and mother; he wants to make her a lover, a lover of God: he is deceiving himself in deceiving her.

But in the midst of all this, and fascinated as she is, she is not, however, so blind as you might believe. Women, even children, are penetrating when they are afraid; they very soon get a glimpse of what may comfort them. This woman, whilst she was dragged at his feet as a frightened yet caressing suppliant, did not fail to notice, through her tears, the emotion she excited. They were both in emotion together—this is to be an accomplice. They both know (without, however, knowing it clearly, but confusedly through instinct and passion) that they have a hold upon each other, she by desire, and he by fear.

Fear has much to do with love. The husband in the middle ages was loved by the wife for his very severity. His humble Griselda recognised in him the right of the paternal rod. The bride of William the Conqueror, having been beaten by him, knew him by this token for her lord and husband. Who has this right in our age? The husband has not preserved it—the priest has it and uses it: he ever holds over woman the rod of authority; he beats her submissive and docile with spiritual rods. But he who can punish, can also pardon; the only one who can be severe, he alone has also what with a timid person is accounted supreme grace—clemency. One word of pardon gains for him instantly, in that poor frightened heart, more than the most worthy would obtain after years of perseverance. Kindness acts just in proportion to the severities and terrors that have preceded it. No seduction is comparable to this.

How can that man be resisted, who, to force one to love him, can entice by the offer of Paradise, or frighten by the terrors of hell? This unexpected return of kindness is a very dangerous moment for her, who, conquered by fear, with her forehead in the dust, expects only the fury of the thunderbolt. What! that formidable judge, that angel of judgment, is suddenly melted! She, who felt already the cold blade of the sword, feels now the warmth of a kind friendly hand, which raises her from the earth. The transition is too great for her; she had still held up against fear, but this kindness overcomes her. Worn out by her alternate hopes and fears, the feeble person becomes weakness itself.

To be able to have all, and then abstain, is a slippery situation! who will keep his footing on this declivity?

Here we find again, in the path of desire, the very point at which we had just now arrived by the path of pride.

Desire, despised at first by pride, as brutal and coarse, turns sophist, and puts before him the terrible problem at which love, mingled with dread, flinches, and turns away his sight. He sees without daring to look, he puts up his hand before his eyes, but with his fingers apart, like the *Vergognosa* of the Campo-Santo.

"Are you sure you possess the heart entirely, if you have not the body? Will not physical possession give up corners of the soul, which otherwise would remain inaccessible? Is spiritual dominion complete, if it does not comprehend the other? The great popes seem to have settled the question: they thought popedom implied empire; and the pope himself, besides his sway over consciences, was king in temporal matters."

Against this sophism of the flesh, the spirit still struggles, and does not fail to answer, "That spiritual conquest, as soon as it is completed in this manner, ceases to be spiritual; that this ambitious conqueror, the spirit, cannot have all without perishing at the moment of victory."

The flesh is not embarrassed; but taking refuge in hypocrisy, makes itself of no importance, and becomes humble to regain its advantage: "Is then the body so important that we should trouble our heads about it? A simple dependent of the soul ought to follow wherever she goes." The mystics are never behindhand, in this matter, in their insults to the body and the flesh. The flesh is the brute animal, says one, which we must cudgel. "Let her pass," says another, "through any muddy brook: what does it signify to the soul that rides above, sublime and pure, without deigning to look down?"

Afterwards comes the vile refinement of the Quietists: "If the inferior part be without sin, the superior grows proud, and pride is the greatest sin:

consequently the flesh ought to sin, in order that the soul may remain humble; sin, producing humility, becomes a ladder to ascend to heaven."

"Sin!—But is it sin? (depraved devotion finds here the ancient sophism:) The holy by its essence, being holiness itself, always sanctifies. In the spiritual man, everything is spirit, even what in another is matter. If, in its superior flight, the holy should meet with any obstacle that might draw it again towards the earth, let the inferior part get rid of it; it does a meritorious work, and is sanctified for it."

Diabolical subtlety! which few avow clearly, but which many brood over, and cherish in their most secret thoughts. Molinos is forgotten, but Molinosism still exists.[2]

Besides, false reasonings are hardly necessary in the miserable state of dreaming in which a soul lives, when deprived of will and reason.

Beside herself, and out of her senses, having lost all connection with reality, ever buried in miracles, intoxicated with God and the devil, she is weakened to death: but the excess of this weakness is yet strong enough to give poison and fever in return; terrible contagion—you thought that this morally dead person would toil after you, but it is you who will follow her: she will bear away the living.

Here end the subtleties with which desire had been satisfied. A horrible light breaks upon them, and sophistry finds no longer any clouds to darken it. You see, then, when it is too late, that you have done more than you wanted. You have destroyed precisely what would have served you; for each of these suppressed powers, the will, the mind, and the heart, which now are no more, would have been for you, had they remained alive. But, alas! they are crushed, faded, and void. The essence of existence once destroyed, no longer feels; it can neither attach itself to anything, nor be captivated by anything. You wanted to bind it fast, but you have stifled it. Now you would wish her, whose life is annihilated, to be alive, or at least to revive. That is a miracle beyond your power. The thing you see, is, and ever will be, a cold shadow, without any life to answer you. Do what you will, you will find no responsive throbbing. This will be your despair. You can feign everything, and say everything, except one word, which we defy you to pronounce without grief—the sacred name of love.

Love! why, you have assassinated it! In order to love, you must have a person; but what was a person you have made a thing. Proud man! you who every day summon your Creator to descend upon the altar, you have inverted the order of creation: you have destroyed a being.

You, who, out of a GRAIN OF CORN, can make a GOD, tell me, was it not also a god that you held just now in that credulous and docile soul? what have you done with that interior god of man, that we call liberty? You have put yourself in its place; in the place of that power, by which man is man, I see nonentity.

Well! that nonentity shall be your torment. You will probe it in vain; however low you penetrate, you will find but a void, nothing, neither *will* nor *power*. There everything that could have loved has perished.

[1] This postponing manoeuvre is admirably calculated to draw from a woman a secret, that does not belong to confession, that she will not tell, her husband's secret, her lover's *real name*, &c., &c. They always get it out of her at last.

[2] This word Molinosism reminds us of an old forgotten system. In practice, it is a thing of all times, an instinct, a blind belief, which is natural to the weak, and which may be thus expressed:—with the strong, everything is right; a saint cannot sin. See the patient, if he is lucky enough to invite his physician to dinner with him: he has recovered his assurance and boldness, and indulges in every dish without being afraid. I believe, moreover, that real Molinosism is always a powerful argument with the simple. A contemporary writer, Llorente, relates (t. iii., ch. 28, article 2, ed. 1817), that when he was secretary to the Inquisition, they brought before that tribunal a capuchin friar, who was director of a community of Beguines, nearly all of whom he had seduced, by persuading them that they were not straying from the road to perfection. He would say to each of them, at the Confessional, that he had received a singular grace from God; "Our Lord," said he, "has deigned to appear to me in the consecrated wafer, and He has said to me, almost all the souls that you direct here are pleasant to Me, but especially such a one (*the capuchin named the one he was then speaking to*). She is already so

perfect that she has overcome every passion, save desire, which is her torment. For this reason, wishing her virtue to be rewarded and that she should serve Me with a quiet mind, I charge you to give her dispensation, but in favour of you; she is to speak of it to no confessor; it would be useless, since with such dispensation she cannot sin." Out of seventeen Beguines, of which the community was composed, this daring capuchin gave dispensation to thirteen, who were discreet for a considerable time; one of them, however, fell ill, expected to die, and revealed all, declaring that she had never been able to believe in the dispensation, but that she had availed herself of it. If the accused party had simply confessed, he would have been let off with a very trifling punishment, the Inquisition being, says Llorente, very lenient towards that kind of offence. But, though he confessed the thing, he maintained that he had acted properly, being empowered by Jesus Christ. "What!" said they, "is it likely that our Lord appeared to you, to exempt you from a precept of the Decalogue." "Why, he exempted Abraham from the fifth commandment, ordering him to kill his son, and the Hebrews from the seventh, ordering them to rob the Egyptians." "Yes, but these were mysteries favourable to religion." "And what then is more favourable to religion than to quiet thirteen virtuous souls, and lead them to a perfect union with the divine essence?" I recollect, says Llorente, saying to him, "But, father, is it not surprising that this singular virtue happened to be precisely in the thirteen young and handsome ones, and never in the four others who were ugly or old?" He replied coldly, "The Holy Spirit inspires as it pleases."

The same author, in the same chapter, though reproaching the Protestants with having exaggerated the corruption of the confessors, avows, "In the sixteenth century, the

Inquisition had imposed upon women the obligation of denouncing guilty confessors, but the denunciations were found to be so numerous, that the penitents were declared to be relieved from denouncing." Trials of this description were conducted with closed doors, and condemnations were hushed up in secret little *autodafés*. From the number of trials which Llorente extracts from the registers, he compares the morals of the different religious orders, and finds, in figures, a very natural result that might be guessed without the help of arithmetic. They deceived their penitents, just in proportion to the more or less money and liberty they had to seduce others with. Poor and secluded monks were dangerous confessors; friars, who had more liberty, and secular priests, seldom made use of the hazardous means of the Confessional; because they found favourable opportunities elsewhere. They who, as directors, see women *tête-à-tête* at home, or in their own houses, have no need to corrupt them at the altar.

PART III.

FAMILIES.

CHAPTER I.

SCHISM IN FAMILIES.—THE DAUGHTER;—BY WHOM EDUCATED.—IMPORTANCE OF EDUCATION, AND THE ADVANTAGE OF THE FIRST INSTRUCTOR.—INFLUENCE OF PRIESTS UPON MARRIAGE, WHICH THEY OFTEN RETAIN AFTER THAT CEREMONY.

The drama which I have endeavoured to sketch does not always, thanks be to God, go so far as the annihilation of the will and personality. One cannot well discern where it stops, owing to the dark cloak of reserve, discretion, and hypocrisy, with which this black community is enveloped. Besides, the clergy have been doubly guarded in their conduct during the present contentions.[1] It is out of the church, in houses, and family circles, that we must seek for what will throw the principal light upon what the Church conceals. Look well; there you see a reflection, unfortunately too clear, of what is passing elsewhere.

We have already said, if you enter a house in the evening, and sit down at the family table, one thing will almost always strike you; the mother and daughters are together, of one and the same opinion, on one side; whilst the father is on the other, and alone.

What does this mean? It means that there is some one more at this table, whom you do not see, to contradict and give the lie to whatever the father may utter. He returns fatigued with the cares of the day, and full of those which are to come; but he finds at home, instead of repose and comfort for the mind, only the struggle with the past.

We must not be surprised at it. By whom are our daughters and wives brought up? We must repeat the expression,—by our enemies, the enemies of the Revolution, and of the future.

Do not cry out here, nor quote me this or that sermon you have preached.

What do I care for the democratical parade which you make in the pulpit, if everything beneath us, and behind us, all your little pamphlets which issue by thousands and millions, your ill-disguised system of instruction, your confessional, the spirit of which now transpires, show us altogether what you are,—the enemies of liberty? You, subjects of a foreign prince; you, who deny the French church, how dare you speak of France?

Six hundred and twenty thousand[2] girls are brought up by nuns under the direction of the priests. These girls will soon be women and mothers, who, in their turn, will hand over to the priests, as far as they are able, both their sons and their daughters.

The mother has already succeeded as far as concerns the daughter; by her persevering importunity, she has, at length, overcome the father's repugnance. A man who, every evening, after the troubles of business and the warfare of the world, finds strife also at home, may certainly resist for a time, but he must necessarily give in at last; or he will be allowed neither truce, cessation, rest, nor refuge. His own house becomes uninhabitable. His wife having nothing to expect at the confessional but harsh treatment, as long as she does not succeed, will wage against him every day and every hour the war they make against her; a gentle one, perhaps; politely bitter, implacable, and obstinate.

She grumbles at the fire-side, is low-spirited at table, and never opens her mouth either to speak or eat; then bed-time, the inevitable repetition of the lesson she has learned, even on the pillow. The same sound of the same bell, for ever and ever; who could withstand it? what is to be done? Give in or become mad!

If the husband were firm, obstinate, and persevering enough to stand this trial, the wife, perhaps, would not resist. "How can I see her so unhappy, pining, uneasy, and ill? She is evidently growing thinner. I had much rather save my wife." Such is the language of the husband. If he be not subdued by his wife, he is by his own heart. The next day the son leaves his college for the *Christian college*, or the school for the little seminary. The daughter is led triumphantly by her mother to the excellent boarding-school close by, where the good abbé confesses and directs. In less than a year the boarding-school is found to be not quite good enough, being still too worldly; the little girl is then given over to the nuns, whose superior our abbé happens to be, in some convent of his, that is, under his protection and his lock and key.

Good-humoured parent, lie easy and sleep sound. Your daughter is in good hands: you shall be contradicted till your death. Your daughter is really a girl of good sense; and on every subject, having been carefully armed against you, will take, whatever you may say, the opposite side of the question.

What is very singular, the father, generally, is aware that they are bringing up his child against him. Man, you surprise me! what do you expect then? "Oh! she will forget it; time, marriage, and the world will wear away all that." Yes, for a time, but only to re-appear; at the first disappointment in the world it will all return. As soon as she grows somewhat in years, she will return to the habits of the child; the master she now has will be her master then, whether for your contradiction, in your old age, good man, or for the despair and daily damnation of her father and husband. Then will you taste the fruit of this education.

Education! a mere trifle, a weak power, no doubt, which the father may, without danger, allow his enemies to take possession of!

To possess the mind, with all the advantage of the first possessor! To write in this book of blank paper whatever they will! and to write what will last for ever! For, remember well, it will be in vain for you to write upon it hereafter; what has once been indited, cannot be erased. It is the mystery of her young memory to be as weak in receiving impressions as it is strong in keeping them. The early tracing that seemed to be effaced at twenty re-appears at forty or sixty. It is the last and the clearest, perhaps, that old age will retain.

What! will not reading, and the press, the great overruling power of our own days, give a stronger education than the former one? Do not rely on this. The influence of the press partly annuls itself; it has a thousand voices to speak, and a thousand others to answer and destroy what it has said. Education does not make so much noise; it does not talk; it reigns. Look, in that little class, without witness, control, or contradiction, a man is speaking; he is master, an absolute master, invested with the most ample power to punish and chastise. His voice, not his hand, has the power of a rod; the little, trembling, and believing creature, who has just left her mother's apron, receives his weighty words, which enter the soft tablet of her memory, and stick into it, like so many nails of iron.

This is true in speaking of the school, but how much more so as regards the church! especially in the case of the daughter, who is more docile and timid, and certainly retains more faithfully her early impressions. What she heard the first time in that grand church, under those resounding roofs, and the words, pronounced with a solemn voice by that man in black, which then frightened her so, being addressed to *herself*,—ah! be not afraid of her ever forgetting them. But even if she could forget them, she would be reminded of them every week: woman is all her life at school, finding in the confessional her school-bench, her schoolmaster, the only man she fears, and the only one, as we have said, who, in the present state of our manners, can threaten a woman.

What an advantage has he in being able to take her quite young, in the convent where they have placed her, to be the first to take in hand her young soul, and to be the first to exercise upon her the earliest severity, and also the earliest indulgence which is so akin to affectionate tenderness,[3] to be the father and friend of a child taken so soon from her mother's arms.

The confidant of her first thoughts will long be associated with her private reveries. He has had an especial and singular privilege which the husband may envy: what?—why, the virginity of the soul and the first-fruits of the will.

This is the man of whom, young bachelors, you must ask the girl in marriage, before you speak to her parents. Do not deceive yourselves, or you will lose all chance. You shake your heads, proud children of the age; you think you can never be induced to humble yourselves so far. All I hope then is, that you may be able to live single, and wed philosophy; otherwise, I can see you, even now, in spite of all your fine speeches, gliding stealthily, sneaking by twilight into the church, and kneeling down before the priest. There they were lying in wait for you, and there they catch you. You had not foreseen it. Now you are a lover, poor young man, and will do whatever they wish.

I only wish that this girl, bought so dearly, may be really yours. But what with that mother and that priest, the same influence, though diminished for a moment, will soon resume its strength. You will have a wife, minus heart and soul, and you will understand, when it is too late, that he who now gives her away knows well how to keep her.[4]

[1] This circumspection would bear carrying a little farther, if we are to judge of it by the public adventures of the Abbés C. and N., who, by-the-by, will not prosper the less on this account, as two others, of high rank, and known to everybody, have already shown.

[2] M. Louandre gives the figure six hundred and twenty-two thousand girls, in his conscientious statistics.—*Revue des Deux-Mondes*, 1844.

[3] What is direction generally?—1st, *Love before love*; it cultivates in the little girl that power which is now awakening, and it cultivates it so well, that on leaving the convent, her parents see the necessity of a speedy marriage to support her, for she is in danger of falling:—2ndly, *Love after love*. An aged female is, in a layman's estimation, an *old*

woman: but according to the priest's, she is a *woman*: the priest begins where the world ends.

[4] Let us add to this chapter a fact, which (being compared with what we have said about ecclesiastical discipline) inclines us to think that the clergy do not lose sight of the girls who are brought up in the convents under their direction. A friend of mine, whose high position and character render his testimony very important, lately told me that, having placed a young relation of his in a convent, he had heard from the nuns *that they sent to Rome* the names of the pupils who distinguished themselves the most. The *centralization* of such private information, about the daughters of the leading families of the Catholic world, must indeed facilitate many combinations, and be of especial service to Ultramontane politics. The Jesù, if it were so, would be a vast marriage office.

CHAPTER II.

WOMAN.—THE HUSBAND DOES NOT CONSOCIATE WITH HIS WIFE.—HE SELDOM KNOWS HOW TO INITIATE HER INTO HIS THOUGHTS.—WHAT MUTUAL INITIATION WOULD BE.—THE WIFE CONSOLES HERSELF WITH HER SON.—HE IS TAKEN FROM HER.—HER LONELINESS AND ENNUI.—A PIOUS YOUNG MAN.—THE SPIRITUAL AND THE WORLDLY MAN.—WHICH OF THE TWO IS NOW THE MORTIFIED MAN.

Marriage gives the husband a single and momentary opportunity to become in reality the master of his wife, to withdraw her from the influence of another, and make her his own for ever. Does he profit by it? Very rarely. He ought, in the very beginning, when he has much influence over her, to let her participate in the activity of his mind, his business, and ideas, initiate her in his projects, and create an activity in her by means of his own.

To wish and think as he does, both acting with him and suffering with him—this is marriage. The worst that may happen is not that she may suffer, but that she may languish and pine away, living apart, and like a widow. How can we wonder, then, if her affection for him be lessened? Ah! if, in the beginning, he made her his own, by making her share his ambition, troubles, and uneasiness:—if they had watched whole nights together, and been troubled with the same thoughts, he would have retained her affections. Attachment may be strengthened by grief itself; and mutual sufferings may maintain mutual love.

Frenchwomen are superior to those of England or Germany, and, indeed, to any other women, in being able not only to assist man, but to become his companion, his friend, his partner, his *alter ego*. None but the commercial classes, generally speaking, are wise enough to profit by this. See, in the shop-keeping quarters, in the dark storehouses of the *Rue des Lombards*, or the Rue de la Verrerie, the young wife, often born of rich parents, who, nevertheless, remains there, in that little glazed counting-house, keeping the books, registering whatever is brought in or taken out, and directing the clerks and porters. With such a partner the house will prosper. The household is improved by it. The husband and wife, separated by their occupations during the day, are the better pleased to unite together in common thought.

Without being able to participate so directly in the husband's activity, the wife might also, in other professions, be able to associate with him in his business, or, at least, in his ideas. What makes this difficult (I have not attempted to disguise it) is the spirit of specialty which goes on increasing in our different professions, as well as in our sciences, and driving us into minute details; whereas woman, being less persevering, and, moreover, less called upon to apply herself with precision, is confined to a knowledge of generalities. The man who will seriously initiate a woman into his own life, can do it safely and completely, if she love him, but he would require to possess both patience and kindness. They have come together, as it were, from the two opposite poles, and prepared by a totally different education. Since it is so, how can you expect that your young wife, intelligent as she is, should understand you at once? If she do not understand you, it is, too frequently, your own fault: this almost always proceeds from the abstract, dry, and scholastic forms which you have imbibed from your education. She, remaining in the sphere of common sense and sentiment, understands nothing of your formulas, and seldom, very seldom, indeed, do you know how to translate them into plain language. This requires address, will, and feeling. You would want, sir, let me tell you, both more sense and more love.

At the first word she does not understand, the husband loses his patience. "She is incapable, she is too frivolous." He leaves her, and all is over. But that day he loses much. If he had persevered, he would gradually have led her along with him; she would have lived his life, and their marriage would have been real. Ah! what a companion he has lost! how sure a confidant! and how zealous an ally! In this person, who, when left to herself, seems to him too trifling, he would have found, in moments of difficulty, a ray of inspiration, and often useful advice.

I am here entering upon a large subject, where I should wish to stop. But I cannot. One word more: the man of modern times, a victim of the division of work, and often condemned to a narrow speciality, in which he loses the sentiment of general life, and becomes a morbid sort of a being, would require to have with him a young and serene mind, more nicely balanced, and less given to specialty than his own, that might lead him from the confined notions of trade, and restore him to the charms of a well-regulated mind. In this age of eager opposition, when the day is taken up with active business, and we return home worn out with toil or disappointment, it is necessary to have a wife at the domestic fire-side to refresh the burning brain of the husband. This workman (what are we all but workmen, each in his own particular line?), this blacksmith, panting with thirst, after beating the iron, would receive from her the living fountain of the beautiful and good, of God and nature; he would drink for a moment of eternal streams. Then he would *forget*, take courage, and breathe freely again. Having been relieved by her, he would in his turn assist her with his powerful hand, lead her into his own world, his own life, his way of progress and new ideas—the way of the future!

Unfortunately this is not the way of the world. I have sought everywhere, but in vain, for this fine exchange of thought, which alone realizes marriage. They certainly try for a moment, in the beginning, to communicate together, but they are soon discouraged: the husband grows dumb, his heart, dried up with the arid influence of interest and business, can no longer find words. At first she is astonished and uneasy: she questions him. But questions annoy him; and she no longer dares to speak to him. Let him be easy; the time is coming when his wife, sitting thoughtful by the fire-side, absent in her turn, and framing her imaginary plans, will leave him in quiet possession of his taciturnity.

First of all, she has a son. It is to him, if he be left to her, that she will devote herself entirely. Should she go out, she gives him her hand, and soon her arm; he is now like a young brother, "a little husband." How tall he has grown already! how quickly time passes; and it is a pity he grows so; for now comes the separation, his Latin and his tears. Must he not become a learned man? Must he not enter, as soon as possible, into the world of violence and opposition, where he will acquire the bad passions which are cultivated so carefully in us, pride, ambition, hatred, and envy? The mother would like to wait longer: "What is the hurry? he is so young, and those schools are so strict! He will learn much better at home, if they will let him remain with her; she will engage masters and superintend his studies herself; she will discontinue going to balls."—"Impossible, madam, impossible! you would make a milksop of him." The fact is, the father, though he likes his son very much, finds, that in a well-regulated house this movement and constant noise and bustle are intolerable. He is unable to support anything of the sort: fatigued, disgusted, and ill-humoured, he wants silence and repose.

Wise husbands, who make so little of the resistance of a mother, do you not perceive that it is also by an instinct of virtue that this woman wishes to keep her son the pure and irreproachable witness, before whom she would always have remained holy? If you knew how useful the presence of the child is to the house, you yourself would desire to keep him. As long as that child remained there, the house was blessed. In his presence how difficult it is to loosen the family tie! What completes marriage and the family? The child, the object of their hopes. Who maintains the family? The child they possess. He is the aim and the end, the mediator—I had almost said the whole.

We cannot repeat it too often, for nothing is more true—woman is alone. She is alone if she has a husband; she is also alone even with a son. Once at school, she sees him only by favour, and often at long intervals. When he leaves school, other prisons await the youth, and other exiles.

A brilliant evening party is given: enter those well-lighted rooms; you see the women sitting in long rows, well-dressed, and entirely alone. Go, about four o'clock, to the Champs-Elysées, and there you will see again the same women, sad and spiritless, on their way to the Bois de Boulogne, each in her own carriage, and alone. These are in a calash, those at the far end of a shop; but all are equally alone.

There is nothing in the life of women, who have the misfortune to have nothing to do, that may not be explained by one single word—loneliness, *ennui*. *Ennui*, which is supposed to be a languishing and negative disposition of the mind, is, for a nervous woman, a positive evil impossible to support. It grasps its prey, and gnaws it to the core: whoever suspends the torment for a moment is considered a saviour.

Ennui makes them receive female friends, whom they know to be inquisitive, envious, slandering enemies. *Ennui* makes them endure novels in newspapers, which are suddenly cut short, at the moment of the greatest interest. *Ennui* carries them to concerts, where they find a mixture of every kind of music, and where the diversity of styles is fatigue for the ear. Ennui drags them to a sermon, which thousands listen to, but which not one of them could bear to read. Nay, even the sickening half-worldly and half-devout productions, with which the neo-Catholics inundate the Faubourg Saint German, will find readers among these poor women, the martyrs of *ennui*. Such delicate and sickly forms can support a nauseous dose of musk and incense; which would turn the stomach of any one in health.

One of these young authors explains, in a novel, all the advantage there is in beginning gallantry by gallant devotion. The proceeding is not new. All I wish is, that those who borrowed it from Tartuffe would not give it to us, without its fair portion of wit and humour.

But they have no great need of it. Women listen to their disguised declarations and ambiguous endearments, as a matter of conscience to earn their salvation. The woman, who, with the most sober friend, would be offended at the very first word of friendship, suffers patiently this double-meaning language of the young Levite. The intelligent woman of experience and the world, who has read and seen much, shuts her eyes to the mischief. If he has but little talent, if he is heavy and uninteresting, yet his intentions are so good! Father [Transcriber's note: Rather?] such a one answers for him; he is an excellent young man.

The fact is, that while he pretends devotion, he speaks of love; this is his merit. Even though it be spoken of in a weak and insipid manner, it is still a merit with her who is no longer young. The husband, however distinguished he may be, has the fault of being a *positive* man, entirely taken up, as they say, with worldly interests. It is very true he is working for the interest of his family; he provides for the future welfare of his children; he consumes his life to support the luxury in which his wife lives, and beyond his fortune.

Perhaps this husband would be justified in saying that all this, however material may be the result, is also for him a moral interest, *an interest of the heart.* Perhaps he might add, that in being engaged with worldly interests in our assemblies and tribunals, besides a thousand other different positions for the profit of others, we may show ourselves to be more *disinterested,* and consequently more spiritualised, than all those *brokers of spirituality* who turn the Church into an exchange.

Let us here point out a contrast which is not sufficiently noticed.

In the middle ages the *priest* was the spiritual and *mortified man.* By the studies to which he alone devoted himself, by nocturnal prayers and vigils, by the excess of fasting, and by monastic flagellations, he mortified his body. But in these days very little remains of all that; the Church has softened down everything. The priests live as others do: if many pass a mean and pitiful life, it is, at least, generally unattended with risk. We see it, moreover, in the freedom of mind with which they engage the leisure of women with interminable conversations.

Who is the mortified man in the present day, in this time of hard work, eager efforts, and fiery opposition? It is the layman, the worldly man. This man of the world, full of cares, works all day and all night, either for his family, or for the State. Being often engaged in details of business or studies, too thorny to interest his wife and children, he cannot communicate to them what fills his own mind. Even at the hour of rest he speaks little, being always pursuing his idea. Success in business and invention in science are only obtained at a high price—the price that Newton mentions, *by ever thinking of it.* Solitary among his kindred, he runs the risk, making their glory, or their fortune, to become a stranger to them.

The Churchman, on the contrary, who, in these days, to judge of him by what he publishes, studies little, and invents nothing, and who no longer wages against himself that war of mortifications imposed by the middle ages, coolly and quietly pursue two very different occupations at the same time. By his assiduity and fawning words, he gains over the family of the man of business, at the very moment he hurls down upon him from the pulpit the thunders of his eloquence.

CHAPTER III.

THE MOTHER.—ALONE, FOR A LONG TIME, SHE CAN BRING UP HER CHILD.—INTELLECTUAL NOURISHMENT.—GESTATION, INCUBATION, AND EDUCATION.—THE CHILD GUARANTEES THE MOTHER.—THE MOTHER GUARANTEES THE CHILD.—SHE PROTECTS ITS NATURAL ORIGINALITY.—PUBLIC EDUCATION MUST LIMIT THIS ORIGINALITY.—EVEN THE FATHER LIMITS IT.—THE MOTHER DEFENDS IT.—MATERNAL WEAKNESS.—THE MOTHER WOULD MAKE HER SON A HERO.—THE HEROIC DISINTERESTEDNESS OF MATERNAL LOVE.

We have already said, if you wish your family to resist the foreign influence which dissolves it, *keep the child at home* as much as possible. Let the *mother* bring it up under the father's direction, till the moment when it is claimed for public instruction by its great mother, its native land. If the mother bring up the child, the consequence will be, that she will always remain by her husband's side, needing his advice, and anxious to receive from him fresh supplies of knowledge. The real idea of a family will here be realised, which is for the child to be initiated by the mother, and the mother by the husband.

The mother's instinct is just and true; it deserves to be respected. She wishes to keep her child: forcibly separated from him at the moment of birth, she is ever seeking to rejoin that part of herself which a cruel violence snatched from her, but which has its root in her heart. When they take it from her to bring it up at a distance, it is a second separation. The mother and the child weep in common, but their tears are disregarded. This is not right. These tears, in which we think we see only weakness, ought not to be disregarded. They show that the child needs her still. Nursing is not yet finished. Intellectual nourishment, like physical food, ought in the beginning to be administered to the child under the form, as it were, of milk, fluid, tepid, mild, and full of life. Woman alone can so give it. Men expect too much at once of this new-born babe, whose teeth, scarcely formed, are painful. They want to give it bread, and they beat it if it does not bite. In God's name give him more milk: he will drink willingly.

Who will believe some future day that men have thus undertaken to nurse and feed these sucklings? Ah! leave them alone to women! A lovely sight to see a child rocked in the arms of a man! Take care, awkward idiot! It is fragile; handling it in your clownish hands you may break it.

This is the dispute between the master and child: man imparts science by methods proper to man, in a state of fixed rules by very precise classifications, with angular, and, as it were, crystallised forms. Well! these crystal prisms, as luminous as they may be, wound by their angles and sharp points. The child, in a soft and tender state, cannot, for a long time, receive anything which has not the fluidity of life. The master grows angry and impatient at the slowness of the pupil, and knows not how to succeed with him. There is but one person in the world who has the delicate perception of the careful management which the child requires, and this one person is she who has borne it, and who forms for ever with it an identical whole. Gestation, incubation, and education, are three words which are long synonymous.

Much longer than people would believe. The influence of the mother over the child, whose faculties are developing, is greater and more decisive than that which she exercised over the suckling infant. I do not know whether it be indispensable for the mother to feed it from her breast; but I am very sure it is necessary that she should nourish it from her heart. Chivalry was perfectly aware that love was the most powerful motive for education. That alone did more in the middle ages to advance humanity than all the disputes of school-divinity have been able to do to retard it.

We also have our school-divinity, the spirit of empty abstractions and verbal disputes: we shall be able to combat its influence only by prolonging that of the mother, associating her with education, and by giving the child a well-beloved teacher. Love, they say, is a great master. This is especially true of the greatest, the deepest, and the purest of all affections.

How blind and imprudent we are! We take the child from its mother at a time when it was most necessary to her. We deprive her of the dear occupation for which God had formed her; and we are afterwards surprised if this woman, cruelly separated, now languishing and idle, give herself up to vain musings; suffer anew the yoke she formerly bore; and, if, as is often the case, fancying herself to remain faithful, she listen to the tempter, who speaks to her in the name of God.

Be prudent, be wise; leave her her son. Woman must ever be loving. Leave her rather the lover whom nature gives her; him whom she would have preferred to all others, whilst you are occupied with your business (with your passions perhaps). Leave on her arm the tall and slender youth, and she will be proud and happy. You fear, lest, having been kept too long by his mother, he may become effeminate. But, on the contrary, if you left her her son, she would become masculine. Try her, she will change, and you will be astonished yourself. Little excursions on foot, and long ones on horseback—no trouble will be too much for her. She begins bravely and heartily the exercises of the young man; she makes herself of his own age, and is born again in this *vita nuova*; even you on your return will think, when you see your Rosalind, that you have two sons.

It is a general rule to which, at least, I have hardly ever seen any exception, that superior men are all the *sons of their mother*. She has stamped upon them, and they reproduce her moral as well as her physical features.

I am about to surprise you. I will tell you that without her he will never be a man. The mother alone is patient enough to develope the young creature, by taking proper care of his liberty. We must be on our guard, and take especial care not to place the child, still too weak and pliable, in the hands of strangers. People of the best intentions, by pressing too much upon him, run the risk of so crushing his faculties, that he will never be able to enjoy the free use of them again. The world is full of men, who remain bondsmen all their lives, from having borne a heavy load too soon. A too solid and too precocious education has injured something within them; their originality, the *genius* and *ingegno*, which is the prime part of man.

Who respects in these days the original and free ingenuity of character, that sacred genius which we receive at our birth? This is almost always the part which offends and gets blamed; it is the reason why "*this boy is not like everybody else.*" Hardly does his young nature awake, and flourish in its liberty, than they are all astonished, and all shake their heads: "What is this? we never saw the like."—Shut him up quickly—stifle this living flower. Here are the iron cages.—Ah! you were blooming, and displaying your luxuriant foliage in the sun. Be wise and prudent, O flower! become dry, and shut up your leaves.

But this poor little flower, against which they are all leagued—what is it, I pray you, but the individual, special, and original element by which this being would have distinguished itself from others, and added a new feature to the great variety of human characters—a genius, perhaps, to the series of great minds. The sterile spirit is almost always that plant which, having been tied too fast to the dead wood which serves to support it, has dried upon it, and gradually become like it; there it is, very regular, and well fastened up, you may fear nothing eccentric from it; the tree is, however, *dead*, and will never bear leaf more.

What do I mean? that the support is useless, and that we must leave the plant to itself? Nothing is further from my thoughts. I believe in the necessity of both educations, that of the family and that of the country. Let us distinguish their influence.

The latter, our public education, which is certainly better in our days than it ever was—what does it require? What is its end and aim? It wishes to harmonise the child with his native land, and with that great country the world. This is what constitutes its legitimacy and necessity. It purposes especially to give him a fund of ideas common to all, to make him a reasonable being, and prevent him from being out of tune with what surrounds him; it hinders him from jarring in the great concert where he is going to take his part, and it checks what may be too irregular in his lively sallies.

So far for public education. Family life is liberty. Yet even here there are obstacles and shackles to his original moral activity. The father regulates this activity: his uneasy foresight imposes on him the duty to bring early this wild young colt to the furrow, where he must soon toil. It too often happens that the father makes a mistake, consults, first of all, his own conveniences, and seeks the profitable and ready traced career, rather than that to which his young and powerful colt was called by nature.

The triumphs of the courser have frequently been lost in the trammels of the riding-school.

Poor liberty! Who then will have eyes to see thee, or a heart to cherish thee? Who will have the patience, the infinite indulgence required to support thy first wanderings, and encourage occasionally what fatigues the stranger, the indifferent person, nay, the father himself? God alone, who has made this creature, and who, having made him, knows him well enough to see and love what is good in him, even in what is bad, God, I say, and with God the mother: for here it is one and the same thing.

When we reflect that ordinary life is so short, and that so many die very young, we hesitate to abridge this first, this best period of life, when the child, free under its mother's protection, lives in Grace, and not in the Law. But if it be true, as I think, that this time, which people believe lost, is precisely the only precious and irreparable period, in which among childish games sacred *genius* tries its first flight, the season when, becoming fledged, the young eagle tries to fly—ah! pray do not shorten it. Do not banish the youth from the maternal paradise before his time; give him one day more; to-morrow, all well and good; God knows it will be soon enough! To-morrow, he will bend to his work and crawl along the furrow. But to-day, leave him there, let him gain full strength and life, and breathe with an open heart the vital air of liberty. An education which is too zealous and restless, and which exacts too much, is dangerous for children. We are ever increasing the mass of study and science, and such exterior acquisitions; but the interior suffers for it. The one is nothing but Latin, the next shines in Mathematics; but where is the *man*, I pray you? And yet it was the *man*, precisely, that was loved and taken care of by the mother. It was man she respected in the wanderings of the child. She seemed to depress her own influence, and even her superintendence, in order that he might act and be both free and strong; but, at the same time, she ever surrounded him as if with an invisible embrace.

There is a peril, I am well aware of it, in this education of love. What love wishes and desires more than all, is to sacrifice itself, and everything else—interests, conveniences, habits, and even life, if necessary. The object of this self-sacrifice may, in his own childish egotism, receive all the sacrifices as a thing due, allow himself to be treated as an inert, motionless idol, and become the more incapable of action, the more they do for him.

This danger is real, but it is counterbalanced by the ardent ambition of the maternal heart, which places, almost always, her best hopes upon her child, and burns to realise them. Every mother of any value, has one firm belief, which is, that her son is destined to be a hero, in action or in science, no matter which. All that has disappointed her expectations in her sad experience of this world will now be realised by this infant. The miseries of the present are already redeemed by the prospect of this splendid future: everything is miserable now; but only let *him* grow, and everything will be prosperous! O poetry! O hope! where are the limits of maternal thought? "I am only a woman, but here is a man: I have given a man to the world." Only one thing perplexes her: will her child be a Bonaparte, a Voltaire, or a Newton?

If, in order to be so, he absolutely must leave her—well! let him go, let him depart from her; she consents to it: if she must tear her own heart-strings, she will. Love is capable of doing everything, even of sacrificing love itself. Yes, let him depart, follow his high destiny, and accomplish the grand dream she had when she bore him in her bosom, or upon her knees. And then, a miracle: this fearful woman, who just before durst not see him walk alone, without fearing he might fall, is become so brave, that she launches him forth in the most dangerous career, on the ocean, or else to that bloody war in Africa. She trembles, she is dying of uneasiness, and yet she persists. What can support her? Her belief that her child cannot perish, since he is destined to be a hero.

He returns. How much he is changed! What! is this fierce soldier my son? He departed a child, and he comes back a man: he seeks to be married. This is another sacrifice, which is not less serious. He loves another! And his mother, in whose heart he is, and ever will be the first, will possess the second place in his affections—alas! a very small place in the moments of his passion. She seeks for, and chooses her own rival: she loves her on his account; she adorns her; she becomes her attendant, and leads her to the altar; and all she asks for there is, that the mother may not be forgotten in the wife!

CHAPTER IV.

LOVE.—LOVE WISHES TO RAISE, NOT TO ABSORB.—THE
FALSE THEORY OF OUR ADVERSARIES, AND THEIR
DANGEROUS PRACTICE.—LOVE WISHES TO FORM FOR
ITSELF AN EQUAL WHO MAY LOVE FREELY.—LOVE IN
THE WORLD, AND IN THE CIVIL WORLD.—LOVE IN
FAMILIES.—LITTLE UNDERSTOOD BY THE MIDDLE
AGES.—FAMILY RELIGION.

Will it be said that, in the preceding chapter, being seduced by a
sweeter subject, I have lost sight of the whole subject in dispute hitherto
pursued in my book?

I think I have, on the contrary, thrown much light upon the question.
Maternal love (that miracle of God) and maternal education enable us to
understand what every education, direction, or initiation ought to be.

The singular advantage which the mother has in education is, that,
being more than all others devoted and disinterested, she respects infantine
personality in the fragile little thing which is becoming a person. She is, for
the child, the defender of his original individuality. She wishes, even at the
expense of her own feelings, that he should act according to his genius, and
that he may grow up and *rise*. What can education and true direction
require? What love desires in its highest and most disinterested idea—that
the young creature may *rise*. Take this word in both its acceptations. She
wishes the child may rise above herself, up to the level of him who helps
her, and even above him, if he can. The stronger party, far from absorbing
the weaker, wishes to make him strong, and put him on an equal footing.
She endeavours to do this by developing in him not only whatever is similar
in their natures, but even whatever is characteristically distinctive between
them, by exciting his free originality, provoking activity in this being born
for action, and by appealing to the person, and what is most personal in the
person, his will. The dearest wish of love is to excite the will, and the moral
force of the person loved, to its highest degree, to heroism!

The ideal of every mother, and it is the true one in education, is to
make a hero, a man powerful in actions and fruitful in works, who may be
endowed with will, power, and a creative genius. Let us compare with this
ideal that of ecclesiastical education and direction.

The latter wishes to make a saint, and *not* a hero; it believes these two words to be diametrically opposite. It is mistaken also in its idea of sanctity, in making it consist not in being in harmony with God, but in absorption in God.

All this priestly theology, as soon as we provoke it a little, and do not allow it to remain in inconsistency, falls headlong down the irresistible declivity, right into this abyss. There it ended, as it was obliged to end, in the seventeenth century. The great directors of that time, who, by being the last, had the advantage of analysing the thing, show us perfectly well the bottom of it, which is annihilation, the art of annihilating activity, the will, and personality. "Annihilate? Yes, but in God." But does God wish it? His active and creating spirit must wish us to resemble Him, to act and to create. You have a wrong idea of God the Father.

This false theory is convicted in practice. By following it closely we have seen that it arrives at quite an opposite goal. It promises to absorb man in God; and it consoles him for this absorption, by promising him that he shall participate in the infinite existence which he is entering. But, in reality, it does nothing more than absorb man in man, in infinite littleness. The person directed being annihilated in the director, of two persons there remains but one; the other, as a person, has perished; and become a thing.

Devout direction, noticed in our first part among the most loyal directors, and among very pious women, gives me two results, which I state thus:—

1st. A saint who discourses for a long time with a female saint on the love of God, infallibly converts her to love.

2nd. If this love remain pure, it is a chance; it is because the man is a saint; for the person directed, losing gradually all her own will, must, in course of time, be at his mercy. We must suppose, also, that he who may do everything will take no advantage of it, and that this miracle of abstinence will be renewed every day. The priest has always thought himself, in his interior strength, to be a great master in matters of love. Accustomed to control his own passions, to be deceitful, and to beat about the bush, he believes he is the exclusive possessor of the real secret how passions are to be managed. He advances under cover of ambiguous expressions, and he advances in safety; for he is patient, and waits till he has gained a footing in habits and in customs. He laughs in his sleeve at our impassioned vivacity, imprudent frankness, and ungoverned impetuosity, which cause us to pass wide of the mark.

If love was the art of surprising the soul, of subjugating it by authority and insinuation, and of conquering it by fear, in order to gain it by indulgence, so that, when wearied and drowsy with exertion, it may allow itself to be enveloped and caught in an invisible net; if this were love, then certainly the priest would be its great teacher.

Clever masters! learn from ignorant and unskilful men, that with all your little arts, you have never known what is this sacred thing. It requires a sincere heart, and loyalty in the means, as its first condition; the second is, that generosity which does not wish to enslave, but rather to set at liberty and fortify what it loves; to love it in liberty, leaving it free to love or not to love.

Come, my saints! and listen to worldly men on this subject: to dramatists, to Molière, and to Shakspeare. These have known more about it than you. The lover is asked who is the loved object? of what name? of what figure? and of what shape? "*Just as high as my heart.*"

A noble standard, which is that of love, as well as that of education, and of every kind of initiation: a sincerely wished-for equality, the desire of raising the other person to one's own height, and of making her one's equal, "Just as high as one's heart." Shakspeare has said so; Molière has done so. The latter was, in the highest degree, "the educating genius;" one who wishes to raise and set free, and who loves in equality, liberty, and intelligence. He has denounced as a crime that unworthy love which surprises the soul by keeping it apart in ignorance, and holding it as a slave and captive.

In his life, conformable to his works, he gave the noble example of that generous love, which wishes that the person loved should be *his equal, and as much as himself,* which strengthens her, and gives her arms even against himself. This is love, and this is faith. It is the belief that sooner or later the emancipated being must return to the most worthy. And who is the most worthy? Is it not he who wished to be loved with liberty?

Nevertheless, let us well weigh the meaning of this important word *his equal,* and all the dangers it may contain. It is as if this creator said to the creature, whom he has made and is now emancipating, "Thou art free; the power under which thou hast grown up holds thee no more: being away from me, and attached to me now only by the heart and memory, thou mayest act and think elsewhere, nay against me if thou wilt!"

This is what is so sublime in love; and the reason why God pardons it so many weaknesses! It is because in this unlimited disinterestedness, wishing to make a free being and to be loved freely by it, it creates its own peril. The saying, "You may act elsewhere," contains also "to love elsewhere," and the chance of losing the object. That hand, so weak before, but now strengthened and made bold by all the cares of affection, receives the sword from love: even would she turn it against him, she can; there is nothing to hinder her, for he has reserved nothing for himself.

Pray let us exalt this idea, and extend it from the love of woman to universal love, to that which makes the life both of the world and of civil society.

In the world, it calls incessantly from kingdom to kingdom the ever-quickening life, which receives the flame, and goes on rising. It raises from unknown depths beings which it emancipates, and arms with liberty, with the power of acting well or ill, and even of acting against him, who creates them, and makes them free.

In the civil world, does love (charity, patriotism, or whatever they call it) do anything but this? Its work is to call to social life and political power whatever is yet without life in the city. It raises up the weak and poor in their rough path, where they crawl on their hands and feet against destiny, and bestows upon them equality and liberty.

The inferior degree of love is a desire to absorb life. Its superior degree is to wish to exalt life in energy and fruitfulness. It rejoices in raising, augmenting, and creating what it loves. Its happiness is to see a new creature of God rise under its influence, and to contribute its aid to the creation, whether it be for good or for ill.

"But is not love, with this disinterestedness, an uncommon miracle? One of those very short instances when the night of our egotism is illumined by a ray from God?"

No, the miracle is permanent. You see it, you have it before your eyes, but you turn away your head. Uncommon, perhaps, in the lover, it is everywhere visible in the mother. Mortal, you seek God in heaven and under the earth, but he is in your own domestic circle.

Man, woman, and child, the unity of the three persons, and their mutual mediation—this is the mystery of mysteries. The divine idea of Christianity is thus to have put the family upon the altar. It placed it there, and there it has left it, for fifteen hundred years. My poor monk, in the middle ages, contemplated it there in vain. He could never understand the mother as initiation. He exhausted his energies by taking the sterile side; he pursued the Virgin, and left us Our Lady.

Man of modern times! thou shalt do what he could not. This shall be thy work. Mayest thou only, in the height of thy abstract genius, not disdain women and children, who will teach thee life! Instruct them in science and the world, and they will speak to thee of God.

Let the family-hearth become firm and strong, then the tottering edifice of religion, political religion, will quietly settle down. Let it never be forgotten, that humble stone, in which we see only our good old domestic Lares, is the corner-stone of the Temple, and the foundation-stone of the City.

ONE WORD TO THE PRIESTS.

I have finished, yet my heart has not. Therefore, one word more.

One word to the priests. I handled them gently, yet they have attacked me. Well! even now, it is not them that I attack. This book is not against them.

It attacks their own slavish state, the unnatural position in which they are kept, and the strange conditions which make them at once unhappy and dangerous: if it has any effect, it will prepare for them the period of deliverance, personal and mental freedom.

Let them say and do what they please, they will not prevent me from being interested in their fate. I impute nothing to them. They are not free to be just, or to love or to hate, they receive the words they are to say, their sentiments and thoughts, from higher powers. They who set them on against me are the same men who are, at this moment, preparing against them the most cruel inquisition. The more insulated and miserable they are made, the greater will be the advantage derived from their restless activity; let them have neither home, family, country, nor heart, if it be possible: to serve a dead system, none but dead men are wanted—wandering and troubled spirits, without a sepulchre and without repose.

By means of the words *unity* and *universal Church*, they have made them quit the ways of the Church of France. They now enjoy the fruits of this change! They well know what Rome is, and what a Jesuitical bishop is. If the universality of mind (which is the only true one) was ever possessed by Rome, she lost it a long time ago; it is to be met with again, in modern times, and it is in France. For two centuries past, we may say, morally speaking, that France is the pope. The authority is here, under one form or another; it is here by Louis XIV., by Montesquieu, Voltaire, and Rousseau, by the *Constituante*, the Code and Napoleon. Europe has always its centre, every other nation is on the outside.

The world goes on, and flies away, far, very far from the middle ages. Most people think of them no more; but I shall not forget them. The shameful parade made of them by any one before my eyes, will not induce me to turn my heart from those dark and mournful ages, with which I have been so long acquainted, suffering when they have suffered. The sympathy I retain for that by-gone age, whose ashes I have warmed again, prevents me from being indifferent to its most faithless representatives. I do not hate, but I make comparisons, and am sad. I cannot pass the front of the church-porch without saying to Nôtre Dame, in the words of the ancient, "O miseram domum, quàm dispari dominaris domino!" Alas! poor house, thou hast made a sad change of masters!

I have never been insensible either to the humiliation of the Church, or to the sufferings of the priest. I have them all present, both before my imagination and in my heart. I have followed this unfortunate man in the career of privations, and in the miserable life into which he is dragged by the hand of a hypocritical authority. And in his loneliness, on his cold and melancholy hearth, where he sometimes weeps at night, let him remember that a man has often wept with him, and that I am that man.

Who would not pity this victim of social contradictions? The laws tell him things diametrically opposite to one another, as if to sport with him. They will and they will not have him obey nature. The canon law says No, and the civil law says Yes. If he take the latter to be serious, the man of the civil law, the judge, whose protection he expects, acts like a priest, seizes him by the robe, and hands him over degraded to the yoke of the canon law. Agree together, then, O laws! and let us be able to find authority somewhere. If this be law, and the other one directly contrary be also law, what will he do, who believes them both to be sacred?

Oh how my heart swells for all these unfortunate men! How many prayers have I made that they may be permitted to abandon a condition, which gives so rude a contradiction to nature and to the progress of the world! Oh! that I might with my hands build up and cheer the domestic hearth of the poor priest, give him the first rights of man, re-establish him in truth and life, and say to him, "Come and sit with us, leave that deadly shadow, and take thy place, O brother, in the sunshine of God!"

Two men have always deeply touched my heart, two solitary beings, two monks—the soldier and the priest. I have seen, often in my thoughts, and always with sadness, these two great sterile armies, to whom intellectual food is refused, or measured out with so niggardly a hand. They whose hearts have been weaned would require to be nourished with the vivifying food of the mind.

What will be the ameliorations and the remedies for these serious evils? We shall not attempt to tell them now. Either means and contrivances are found out by time, or it manages to do without them.

What we may safely say is, that one day or other, these terms *priest* and *soldier* will indicate two ages, rather than two conditions. The word *priest*, in its origin, meant *old man*; a young priest is a nonsensical contradiction.

The soldier is the youth who, after the school of childhood, and that of work, comes to be proved in the great national school of the army, and to gain strength, before he settles down to the quiet state of matrimony and the family table. Military life, when the state has made it what it ought to be, will be the last education, varied with studies, voyages, and perils, the experience of which will be of advantage to the new family which the man will form on his return.

The priest, on the contrary, in the highest acceptation of the term, ought to be an old man, as he was at first, or at least a man of a mature age, who, having passed through the cares of this world, and being well acquainted with family life, has been taught by his experience to understand the sense of the Great Family of the Universe. Seated among the old men, like the elders of Israel, he would communicate to the young the treasures of his experience; he would be the man for all parties; the man who belongs to the poor, the conciliating umpire to prevent lawsuits, and the physician of health to prevent diseases. To be all that, something more is required than an excitable, hot-headed young man. It ought to be a man who has seen, learned, and suffered much, and who has at last found in his own heart the kind words which may comfort us on our way to the world to come.

Milton Keynes UK
Ingram Content Group UK Ltd.
UKHW052104300624
444882UK00004B/280

9 789362 097248